2001

W9-CRS-040

ENGLISH
BIG 8 REVIEW

NYS ENGLISH / LANGUAGE ARTS
8TH GRADE TEST

Author:

Anne Coen McCabe

John Jay High School
Hopewell Junction, NY 12533

Editors:

Wayne Garnsey
Paul Stich

N&N Publishing Company, Inc.

18 Montgomery Street   Middletown, New York 10940-5116

www.nn4text.com   email: nn4text@warwick.net
(800) NN 4 TEXT

NO PERMISSION HAS BEEN GRANTED BY N&N PUBLISHING COMPANY, INC TO REPRODUCE ANY PART OF THIS BOOK BY ANY MECHANICAL, PHOTOGRAPHIC, OR ELECTRONIC PROCESS.

Dedication

Dedicated to Bill, Sheila, Tom, Kevin, Siobhan, and Adelle
who inspire me with faith in the future.

Special Credits

Thanks to my many colleagues who have contributed
their knowledge, skills, and years of experience to the making of our endeavor.
To these educators, our sincere thanks for their assistance
in the preparation of this manuscript:

Timothy Bermingham
William McCabe
Mary Quinn
Barbara Searle
Kathleen Veit

Reference

Top-rate references are most important to consistency in wording. We are grateful to the authors, editors, contributors, and publishers of this excellent resource: *The American Heritage Dictionary*© for fundamental definitions and appropriate word usage [available on CD-ROM through SoftKey Multimedia Inc, Cambridge, MA].

Disclaimer

During the production of this book, all reasonable care was given to follow as closely as possible both the intent and the format, guidelines, frameworks, assessments, and rubric evaluations for the NYS 8th Grade English Language Arts Assessments as released by the University of the State of New York, The State Education Department, Albany, NY 12234. In addition, some portions of *New York State Testing Program, English Language Arts – Test Sampler Draft* [a publication developed through a partnership between the NYS Education Department and CTB/McGraw-Hill, 20 Ryan Ranch Road, Monterey, CA 93940, and copyrighted by CTB/McGraw-Hill] was reviewed and some testing material modified for incorporation in this book. These portions of the "Test Sampler Drafts" provided examples of the types of questions, the formatting, and the scoring guides being developed by or at the direction of the New York State Education Department.

No part of this book may be reproduced by any mechanical, photographic, or electronic process, nor may it be stored in a retrieval system, transmitted, or otherwise copied for public or private use, without written permission from the publisher.

The use of copyrighted material in this book from sources other than N&N Publishing does not constitute review or endorsement by the copyright holder of that material.

© Copyright 1999, 2001
N&N Publishing Company, Inc.
18 Montgomery Street   Middletown, New York 10940
www.nandnpublishing.com   (800) NN4 TEXT   email: nn4text@warwick.com

Soft Cover Edition: ISBN # 0-935487 67 0
2 3 4 5 6 7 8 9 0 BMP 2009 2008 2007 2006 2005 2004 2003 2002 2001

Printed in the United States of America, BookMart Press, NJ
SAN # 216 - 4221

NO PERMISSION HAS BEEN GRANTED BY N&N PUBLISHING COMPANY, INC TO REPRODUCE ANY PART OF THIS BOOK BY ANY MECHANICAL, PHOTOGRAPHIC, OR ELECTRONIC PROCESS.

PAGE 2   *ENGLISH – BIG 8 REVIEW* (ENGLISH / LANGUAGE ARTS 8TH GRADE TEST) N&N©

TABLE OF CONTENTS

NO PERMISSION HAS BEEN GRANTED BY N&N PUBLISHING COMPANY, INC TO REPRODUCE ANY PART OF THIS BOOK BY ANY MECHANICAL, PHOTOGRAPHIC, OR ELECTRONIC PROCESS.

NO PERMISSION HAS BEEN GRANTED BY N&N PUBLISHING COMPANY, INC TO REPRODUCE ANY PART OF THIS BOOK BY ANY MECHANICAL, PHOTOGRAPHIC, OR ELECTRONIC PROCESS.

PREFACE

MAKING A NAME FOR MYSELF

Who am I? How can I answer that? My name is one answer. I may choose to use the name that the adults in my life chose for me, or I may choose to use a name that my friends and I have agreed upon. However, those words, my name, are special to me.

Words do have something to do with identifying who I am. Words other than my name also have special meaning to me. I have a need to let people know who I am, what I think, and what I want. Language allows me to do this in an impressive and clear way.

The better I am with language, the better my chances are for influencing other people and advancing in this world. To increase my chances of becoming better with language, the New York State Regents has designed a test at the end of eighth grade. It will measure my ability to understand language and use language to convey my understanding. This test will help others to determine how much assistance I will need in order to successfully master language skills.

JOHNNY HANCOCK

Child-like

John Hancock

Evolving Style

John Hancock

sophisticated

No matter what my present language skills are, I can begin now to make a name for myself. Just as I can practice writing my signature so that it looks the way I want it to, so I can practice my language skills until they also present me the way I want others to see me. I need not be stuck signing checks using a large crayon and printing in childish letters; I can practice and improve. So too, I need not remain at my current skill level of language. I can practice and improve. I want to make a name for myself.

I want to be somebody special. I want respect. I can start today.

NO PERMISSION HAS BEEN GRANTED BY N&N PUBLISHING COMPANY, INC TO REPRODUCE ANY PART OF THIS BOOK BY ANY MECHANICAL, PHOTOGRAPHIC, OR ELECTRONIC PROCESS.

NO PERMISSION HAS BEEN GRANTED BY N&N PUBLISHING COMPANY, INC TO REPRODUCE ANY PART OF THIS BOOK BY ANY MECHANICAL, PHOTOGRAPHIC, OR ELECTRONIC PROCESS.

LEARNING STANDARDS

The 8th grade testing program in New York State uses four English Language Arts Learning Standards as focal points. They help students understand the various needs for and uses of language. These standards are:

- Students will listen, speak, read, and write for **information and understanding**.

- Students will listen, speak, read, and write for **literary response and expression**.

- Students will listen, speak, read, and write for **critical analysis and evaluation**.

- Students will listen, speak, read, and write for **social interaction**.

Language is a unified whole. In reality, it cannot be separated into these neat compartments. However, these standards are a practical way to discuss the needs and value of language. By using the standards, the New York Board of Regents can focus on certain skills and create rubrics (scoring guides) by which my work is evaluated and ultimately improved.

I will begin preparing for my evaluation by studying the standards to be assessed in the main tasks of the test. I will first be introduced to the blueprint of the test, and then I will work through some discussion and practice of the skills involved. The small "road sign" icons above will remind me of the standard being assessed. The detailed meaning of the icons will appear as I begin working on the actual tasks of the test.

NO PERMISSION HAS BEEN GRANTED BY N&N PUBLISHING COMPANY, INC TO REPRODUCE ANY PART OF THIS BOOK BY ANY MECHANICAL, PHOTOGRAPHIC, OR ELECTRONIC PROCESS.

NO PERMISSION HAS BEEN GRANTED BY N&N PUBLISHING COMPANY, INC TO REPRODUCE ANY PART OF THIS BOOK BY ANY MECHANICAL, PHOTOGRAPHIC, OR ELECTRONIC PROCESS.

BLUEPRINT

THE 8TH GRADE TEST BLUEPRINT

The blueprint or plan of New York State English Language Arts Test for Grade 8 calls for dividing the work into two Sessions – the first is 90 minutes, and the second is 60 minutes. The chart that follows will help me understand what I can expect during the test.

Session	Texts	Response Format	Standards & Purposes
Session 1 (90 Min.)	3 - 5 reading passages 1 listening passage	26-28 multiple choice questions 3 short responses 1 extended response	**Standards 1 & 2** To assess ability to: • Read literary and informational texts • Understand and interpret important ideas and information • Recognize literary elements and their effect • Interpret vocabulary in context **Standard 2** • Listen to an informational text • Select and interpret important ideas and information • Demonstrate understanding of passages in detailed responses to questions • Synthesize understandings in well-developed extended response, following the conventions of standard written English
Session 2 (60 Min.)	2 linked passages (1 informational and 1 literary, or 2 literary) 1 writing prompt	3 short responses 1 extended response	**Standards 2 & 3** To assess ability to: • Read 2 texts from different genres • Select important ideas and information • Understand literary elements and their effect • Demonstrate understanding of passages in detailed responses to questions • Synthesize understandings in well-developed extended response, following the conventions of standard written English • Create well-developed expressive and expository responses to a given task, using knowledge of literary elements and expository structures and following the conventions of standard written English

NO PERMISSION HAS BEEN GRANTED BY N&N PUBLISHING COMPANY, INC TO REPRODUCE ANY PART OF THIS BOOK BY ANY MECHANICAL, PHOTOGRAPHIC, OR ELECTRONIC PROCESS.

NO PERMISSION HAS BEEN GRANTED BY N&N PUBLISHING COMPANY, INC TO REPRODUCE ANY PART OF THIS BOOK BY ANY MECHANICAL, PHOTOGRAPHIC, OR ELECTRONIC PROCESS.

SCORING THE TEST

Now that I have seen the NYS Standards, I understand the 8th Grade English Test will focus on the first three standards. The Fourth Standard, social interaction, receives less emphasis on the 8th Grade English Test. The Board of Regents hopes that by achieving the better communications fostered by the first three standards, improved social interaction among citizens will result. I should get used to seeing the icons which represent the standards. When I see the icon for a standard, I know that this standard is the focus of the task on which I am working.

HOW THE TEST IS SCORED

As the test "Blueprint" shows, there are three types of tasks (responses) on the 8th Grade English Test: 26-28 multiple choice questions, 6 short responses (3 in each of the two sessions), and 2 extended responses (1 in each of the two sessions). To do my best on the test, I must understand how the test will be scored.

SESSION 1

Typical Directions: In this part of the test, you are going to read an article, a story, and an essay, and answer questions about what you have read. You may look back at the reading selections as often as you like.

After reading the selections, I must answer a series of multiple choice questions about the reading passage. I must select the best answer from those given. My choices will be scored "right" or "wrong" on these 26-28 multiple choice questions.

At the end of Session 1, I will listen to two passages and take notes. Then I will fill in a graphic organizer chart, write two short and one extended responses. For the extended question, I am given a special space to plan my writing and a lined page for writing my finished response. My short and extended response answers for the listening questions are scored on special "qualities" which make up the New York State assessment **rubric** (set of official rules). I will be judged on my ability to:

- **show a clear understanding of the task** including making some reference to the text and/or visual part of the question,

- **develop my response factually and convincingly,**

- **organize my writing clearly** using proper introduction, body, and conclusion with smooth transition,

- **use vocabulary appropriately,** and

- **apply the rules of Standard English writing**.

NO PERMISSION HAS BEEN GRANTED BY N&N PUBLISHING COMPANY, INC TO REPRODUCE ANY PART OF THIS BOOK BY ANY MECHANICAL, PHOTOGRAPHIC, OR ELECTRONIC PROCESS.

SESSION 2

Typical
Directions: In this part of the test, you are going to read an article and a poem. First you will answer questions on what you have read. You may look back at the article and poem as often as you like. Then you will be asked to write an essay.

In Session 2, I will read two literary passages and fill in a graphic organizer chart, write two short responses, and write an extended response that compares the two passages. Finally, I must write an "independent writing" extended response generally connected to a theme related to the two passages. For the extended questions, I am given a special space to plan my writing and a lined page for writing my finished responses.

THE 5 QUALITIES OF THE NYS ENGLISH EIGHT SCORING RUBRIC	
Meaning	I will be graded in part on my ability to understand what I read in the text and visuals. Reading is one of the things which I can do outside class to enhance my language ability. In addition to school-assigned readings, I should try to read other works of interest for at least fifteen minutes a day. If I do this and also do my assigned reading, I will probably notice an improvement in my reading level.
Development	I will be graded on how well I express my ideas. I must elaborate on my ideas, using specific and relevant details and examples to support my statements. I must be precise (exact) in my response to the task (question). I must make specific references to facts in the text and/or visuals of the task.
Organization	I will be graded on how I "put together" my writing so that it makes sense to the reader. Here is where my knowledge of the writing process will be of great value. The organizational procedures that I have learned include: pre-writing; use of introductory, body, and conclusion elements; and proofreading and revising.
Language Use	I will be graded on how well my writing shows that I am aware of my audience (reader to whom I am writing) and the purpose of my writing. To show this quality in my writing, I will need to use words effectively, have good sentence structure, and use a variety of sentences.
Conventions	I will be graded on how well I use the rules of the language road. These include punctuation, mechanics, usage, spelling, or just the general term "grammar."

NO PERMISSION HAS BEEN GRANTED BY N&N PUBLISHING COMPANY, INC TO REPRODUCE ANY PART OF THIS BOOK BY ANY MECHANICAL, PHOTOGRAPHIC, OR ELECTRONIC PROCESS.

DESCRIBING THE RUBRIC QUALITIES

To be sure my responses are properly judged, scorers use a rubric based on five qualities (see chart on opposite page). The qualities are Meaning, Development, Organization, Language Use and Conventions. I must pay attention to these qualities in each of the writing response questions in Sessions 1 and 2.

THE KEYS TO SUCCESSFUL WRITING

Here are the steps of the writing process. I must review them and use them whenever I write. These steps help me to understand and follow the process. I know that the writing process is part of the New York State Standards.

Big 8 Advice

THE WRITING PROCESS

I.   Know my task.

II.   Have a clear sense of my audience.

III. Be aware of what I already know about the task and what more I need to know.

IV.   Group my ideas.

V.   Delete those ideas that don't seem related or valuable.

VI.   Organize my groups and include an introduction and conclusion.

VII. Write a first draft.

VIII. Proofread and edit my draft.

IX.   Revise.

X.   Write my final draft.

My teachers stress that the two most essential keys to successful writing are (1) **understanding my audience** and (2) **organizing my task** so that it will be clearly understood. The **Task-Audience Check List** is a way of doing just that.

The Task–Audience check list specifies the major points that I should consider when proofreading your short and extended responses on the English Grade 8 Test.

NO PERMISSION HAS BEEN GRANTED BY N&N PUBLISHING COMPANY, INC TO REPRODUCE ANY PART OF THIS BOOK BY ANY MECHANICAL, PHOTOGRAPHIC, OR ELECTRONIC PROCESS.

In addition, this method will succeed in helping to make me attentive to the primary concerns in editing any piece of writing.

Below is The TASK–AUDIENCE check list. It has been designed to improve my proofreading. I will use it to check over my short and extended responses on the English Grade 8 Test.

Big 8 Advice

Task-Audience Check List

- ✔ ☐ **T**ask is this writing job on which I must focus.
- ✔ ☐ **A**udience consists of any reader other than me.
- ✔ ☐ **S**elect my best ideas to share with my audience.
- ✔ ☐ **K**eep my ideas organized by reviewing my outline.
- ✔ ☐ **A**void using contractions.
- ✔ ☐ **U**se an introduction which includes a motivator sentence (interesting kick-off), a bridge sentence (connection between the motivator and the thesis), and a thesis statement (main point).
- ✔ ☐ **D**evelop the body of my essay by explaining my thesis.
- ✔ ☐ **I**nvolve the reader by offering proof such as simple facts and quotations.
- ✔ ☐ **E**very paragraph must have a topic sentence.
- ✔ ☐ **N**ever jump from idea to idea – use transitions properly.
- ✔ ☐ **C**hoose words which are specific and alive.
- ✔ ☐ **E**nd the essay with a conclusion.

NO PERMISSION HAS BEEN GRANTED BY N&N PUBLISHING COMPANY, INC TO REPRODUCE ANY PART OF THIS BOOK BY ANY MECHANICAL, PHOTOGRAPHIC, OR ELECTRONIC PROCESS.

READING COMPREHENSION

Session I of the test has two parts. The first part consists of the reading comprehension questions – questions that determine whether I understand the reading. There are three to five reading passages, each followed by several reading comprehension questions. Standards 1 and 2 are evaluated by this section of the test. The goal is to assess my ability to:

- read literary and informational texts
- understand and interpret important ideas and information
- recognize literary elements and their effect
- interpret vocabulary in context.

I have a lot of work to do now to review for this part of the exam, so I had better get started.

VOCABULARY FOR READING COMPREHENSION QUESTIONS

1. **literary**: (adj.) having to do with literature, which is writing that does more than merely give information
2. **informational**: (adj.) having to do with facts; factual
3. **text**: (n.) piece of writing
4. **interpret**: (v.) to find the meaning of
5. **element**: (n.) part
6. **effect**: (n.) result (v.) to result
7. **context**: (n.) the words and sentences surrounding a word that help to determine the meaning of the individual word
8. **narrator**: (n.) storyteller
9. **purpose**: (n.) reason for doing something
10. **argument**: (n.) a reason or group of reasons for holding an opinion, a debate, or a quarrel
11. **advice**: (n.) suggestion
12. **essay**: (n.) a type of writing in which an author states his or her opinions
13. **differ**: (v.) contrast with
14. **view**: (n.) way of looking at a thing or at life
15. **inference**: (n.) judgment based on what is suggested rather than said

NO PERMISSION HAS BEEN GRANTED BY N&N PUBLISHING COMPANY, INC TO REPRODUCE ANY PART OF THIS BOOK BY ANY MECHANICAL, PHOTOGRAPHIC, OR ELECTRONIC PROCESS.

I will now study these words by getting some 3"x5" index cards. I will put the word and its part of speech on one side of the card and the meaning on the other side. After I have studied the words, I will try the following practice.

VOCABULARY PRACTICE

Directions: If the word is used correctly in the sentence, put "OK" on the line at the end of the sentence. If the word is used incorrectly, put "No" on the line. For each "No" response, write a new sentence using the word correctly.

1. Great <u>literary</u> works include facts but also stir the soul to think about the meaning of life. _____

    _____

    _____

2. Although the teacher didn't accuse me of cheating, I made that <u>inference</u> based on the fact that he stood next to me, looked me in the eye, and said, "Keep your eyes on your own paper." _____

    _____

    _____

3. Can you <u>interpret</u> him and ask him when he will be finished because I can't wait any longer? _____

    _____

    _____

4. One of the <u>elements</u> of good, active reading is the habit of asking questions as I read. _____

    _____

    _____

5. A <u>recipe</u> is an informational piece of writing. _____

    _____

    _____

6. I failed my road <u>text</u> because I couldn't parallel park. _____

    _____

    _____

NO PERMISSION HAS BEEN GRANTED BY N&N PUBLISHING COMPANY, INC TO REPRODUCE ANY PART OF THIS BOOK BY ANY MECHANICAL, PHOTOGRAPHIC, OR ELECTRONIC PROCESS.

7. The author of that <u>essay</u> clearly indicated what his idea was about pollution. _____

_____

_____

8. Do you think that Dirk will <u>purpose</u> to Buffy? _____

_____

_____

9. The person who tells the story is the <u>narrator</u>. _____

_____

_____

10. The <u>effect</u> of rain on silk or leather is damaging. _____

_____

_____

PERFECTING READING & WRITING SKILLS

I can read, but sometimes I miss the answers to the comprehension questions. I need to read better. Here are some ways that I have found to help me improve.

VISUALS – AN IMPORTANT PART OF READING

When I use a computer as a word processor, I know that I have to place things on the page, and everything on the page is important. This is also true for reading. How things appear on the page can provide easy access to what is important in the reading.

- First, I look at the visuals. If there are pictures, I look at them carefully and read the captions. If there are charts or graphs, I study them carefully. Even boxed information is important. I carefully look at everything on the page before I start to read the text.

- Then, I look at the font, the size, color, and type of print. Words which are in *italics*, **bold print**, <u>underlined</u>, or CAPITALIZED are printed that way so that I will pay special attention to them. I should be sure to do that.

- Next, I look at the way the page uses space. I look for words which are

 centered on the page

NO PERMISSION HAS BEEN GRANTED BY N&N PUBLISHING COMPANY, INC TO REPRODUCE ANY PART OF THIS BOOK BY ANY MECHANICAL, PHOTOGRAPHIC, OR ELECTRONIC PROCESS.

and I look for words which have lines skipped before and after them such as

skipped line ➡ this line. ↖ *skipped line*

All of these are ways in which an author tries to get me to pay special attention to key words.

- For Example, "Directions" is one key word which I cannot afford to ignore. I must read and carefully follow the directions for each part of the test.

Indentations are also very helpful in finding key ideas. I know that every time that an author changes focus, he/she must indent at the beginning of a paragraph. These indentations help me to keep my focus and follow the author's ideas from one to the next. Once I see some part of a piece of writing set off as a paragraph, I can identify a new, important idea.

SENSING HOW NOUNS & PRONOUNS ARE USED

Nouns name persons, places, things, and ideas. Nouns naming particular people places, things, and ideas are **proper nouns**. Nouns naming non-specific people, places, things, and ideas are **common nouns**. Proper nouns are always capitalized.

Finding nouns can help me to find the topic of a piece of writing. Repeated words or synonyms (words which mean the same as) for the nouns emphasize key ideas. I'll try that now. Here are some practice paragraphs that will help me sharpen my reading skills.

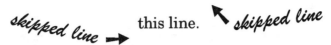

NOUN PRACTICE

Here is a quotation from President Franklin Delano Roosevelt (1933-1945). It appears on one of the walls of his memorial in Washington, D.C.

Directions: Find and <u>underline</u> the twelve (12) nouns in the quotation.

I have seen war. I have seen war on land and sea. I have seen blood

running from the wounded...I have seen cities destroyed...I have seen

children starving. I have seen the agony of mothers and wives. I hate

war.

NO PERMISSION HAS BEEN GRANTED BY N&N PUBLISHING COMPANY, INC TO REPRODUCE ANY PART OF THIS BOOK BY ANY MECHANICAL, PHOTOGRAPHIC, OR ELECTRONIC PROCESS.

In the Roosevelt quotation, what noun (naming word) is repeated three times? "War" is repeated because war is the key idea of this paragraph.

I should also look for words which are used to replace nouns as "namers." Those words are called **pronouns**. The noun which the pronoun is replacing is called the **antecedent**.

Example: **Ed parked his Harley™ on the side street to keep it safe.**
(*Ed* is the noun antecedent of the pronoun *his* and *Harley* is the noun antecedent for the pronoun *it*.)

PRONOUN AND ANTECEDENT PRACTICE

Here is an exercise to sharpen my ability to pick out antecedents.

Directions: Find and <u>underline</u> the eight (8) pronouns in the paragraph below.

The great experiment that is the United States results from a belief in the ability of individuals to put aside all the things which separate them as people long enough to remember the qualities which bind them together as people. Then the many individual differences serve to enhance (add to) the tapestry of the republic. Americans need to recall how the greatest treasure of the nation is its ability to see beyond itself and to fulfill a greater dream which values the vast beauty of individual diversity and uniqueness.

Directions: For each one of the pronouns found and underlined in the paragraph above, find and write the pronoun's antecedent on the line at the right.

Pronoun	Antecedent
1. that	_____
2. which	_____
3. them	_____
4. which	_____
5. them	_____
6. its	_____
7. itself	_____
8. which	_____

NO PERMISSION HAS BEEN GRANTED BY N&N PUBLISHING COMPANY, INC TO REPRODUCE ANY PART OF THIS BOOK BY ANY MECHANICAL, PHOTOGRAPHIC, OR ELECTRONIC PROCESS.

ENGLISH – BIG 8 REVIEW (ENGLISH / LANGUAGE ARTS 8TH GRADE TEST) N&N©   **Page 19**

JOBS & TYPES OF PRONOUNS

Here is a listing of commonly used pronouns.

Some pronouns come in forms which show whether the pronoun is doing the subject job in a sentence (nominative case), the action receiving job in the sentence (objective case), or the showing ownership job (possessive case). The word case shows the form that the pronoun takes because of the job it is doing in the sentence.

Personal Pronouns					
Nominative Case		Objective Case		Possessive Case	
singular	plural	singular	plural	singular	plural
I	we	me	us	mine	ours
you	you	you	you	yours	yours
he, she, it	they	him, her, it	them	his, hers, its	theirs

Relative Pronouns		
Nominative Case	Objective Case	Possessive Case
who	whom	whose
whoever	whomever	
whosoever	whomsoever	

These other pronouns do not show by their spelling what job they are doing in a sentence. In other words, the following pronouns have no case.

Other Pronouns					
this*	which	one	nobody	somebody	ourselves
that*	each	everyone	anyone	myself	yourselves
these*	either	everybody	anybody	yourself	themselves
those*	neither	no one	someone	who	what
himself	herself	few	many	most	much
itself	anything	everything	nothing	something	all
both	any	several	another	none	some

*Demontrative pronouns identify one or more persons or things that are near (*this, these*) or far away (*that, those*).

NO PERMISSION HAS BEEN GRANTED BY N&N PUBLISHING COMPANY, INC TO REPRODUCE ANY PART OF THIS BOOK BY ANY MECHANICAL, PHOTOGRAPHIC, OR ELECTRONIC PROCESS.

Use of Nouns & Pronouns in Topic Sentences

In the quotation from President Roosevelt (page 18), there are seven pronouns – all of which are "I." The antecedent of all of these "I" pronouns is the speaker, Franklin Delano Roosevelt. I know for sure that he is making a point about war.

Now I need to know which of the sentences is in charge of the paragraph, the one sentence which is the topic sentence. I look at all of the **predicates** in the sentences; the predicates are the words which tell how the main noun (the subject) is or what action it is performing. In the quotation from President Roosevelt, the predicates are:

- "have seen" (used 6 times)

- "hate"

The main idea here is that President Roosevelt hates war because of all that he has seen. Looking for repeated nouns or pronouns and finding the predicates will help me to sharpen my skills as a reader.

Reading Comprehension Review

Here are two exercises to bring together many of the skills associated with reading comprehension.

Directions: Read the following passage. For Questions 1 through 5, identify each underlined word(s) as a noun, pronoun, or predicate).

According to author <u>William Edwards</u>, there <u>are</u> at least three essential qualities of most traditional folk heroes. The first quality of a traditional folk hero is representing the values of <u>his/her</u> community. Some of <u>these</u> traditional community values are a willingness to sacrifice for the community, the <u>ability</u> to endure pain and not complain, and the ability to exercise intelligence.

1. <u>William Edwards</u> _____
2. <u>are</u> _____
3. <u>his/her</u> _____
4. <u>these</u> _____
5. <u>ability</u> _____

NO PERMISSION HAS BEEN GRANTED BY N&N PUBLISHING COMPANY, INC TO REPRODUCE ANY PART OF THIS BOOK BY ANY MECHANICAL, PHOTOGRAPHIC, OR ELECTRONIC PROCESS.

READING COMPREHENSION: READING IN CONTEXT PRACTICE

Understanding vocabulary is important on a test. Since I cannot use a dictionary on the test, I have to train myself to look for hints within the passage to estimate the meaning of a difficult word. This is what my teacher calls "reading in context." The next exercise will help me review this skill.

Directions: Read the passage again. For Questions 1 through 5, estimate the meaning of the word from the passage.

According to author William Edwards, there are at least three essential qualities of most **traditional** folk heroes. The first **quality** of a traditional folk hero is to embody the **values** of his/her community. Some of these traditional **community** values are a willingness to sacrifice for the community, the ability to **endure** pain and not complain, and the ability to exercise intelligence.

1.   **traditional** _____

_____

2.   **quality** _____

_____

3.   **values** _____

_____

4.   **community** _____

_____

5.   **endure** _____

_____

NO PERMISSION HAS BEEN GRANTED BY N&N PUBLISHING COMPANY, INC TO REPRODUCE ANY PART OF THIS BOOK BY ANY MECHANICAL, PHOTOGRAPHIC, OR ELECTRONIC PROCESS.

WRITING

The second part of Session 1 and all of Session 2 of the test require me to write responses of different lengths. There are three short responses and one extended response to two listening passages at the end of Session 1. In Session 2, there are three short responses to two linked literary passages and an extended response. Standards 1, 2, and 3 are evaluated by this section of the test. My responses must show I understand the passages and the writing tasks. I must use the details of the passages to make a clear, well organized response. My spelling, grammar, and punctuation will also count in the scoring (see rubrics, pages 118-119).

SENTENCE STRUCTURE

BUILDING SENTENCES FROM CLAUSES & PHRASES

Sentences express complete thoughts. When building a sentence in English, there are four structures from which to choose. Understanding these structures will help me to avoid writing run-ons and fragments. Also, if I understand how a sentence is built, I can learn when and where to place commas. All of this should really improve my performance on the test.

I need to review clauses and phrases. A **clause** is a group of words that has a subject and a predicate. A **phrase** is a group of related words that does not include both a subject and a predicate (e.g., at the movies). For any sentence of any type, there must be at least one **main clause** (a complete, independent thought; a subject and predicate that stand alone). A **subordinate clause** is an incomplete thought that must be used with a main clause to make sense.

Example: **Howard goes to science fiction movies** (main clause) **when he has money** (subordinate clause).

NO PERMISSION HAS BEEN GRANTED BY N&N PUBLISHING COMPANY, INC TO REPRODUCE ANY PART OF THIS BOOK BY ANY MECHANICAL, PHOTOGRAPHIC, OR ELECTRONIC PROCESS.

THE SIMPLE SENTENCE

There is *only one* main clause in a **simple sentence**. Remember that it is not possible to judge sentence type based on length alone.

Examples: **She is.**

("She is." – the one main clause)

In the early part of the day at the top of the hill by the barn, the rooster crowed.

("...the rooster crowed." – the one main clause)

("In the early part...by the barn," – series of prepositional phrases modifying the predicate)

THE COMPOUND SENTENCE

There are *at least two* main clauses in a **compound sentence**; the last *two* of these clauses are joined by a coordinating conjunction preceded by a comma. Coordinating conjunctions include: and, but, or, nor, for, yet, and so.

Examples: **She is, and I am too.**

("She is," and "I am too." – the two main clauses)

In the early part of the day at the top of the hill by the barn, the rooster crowed, and the noise awakened Adelle, our new granddaughter.

("...the rooster crowed, ..." and "...the noise awakened Adelle, ..." – the two main clauses)

THE COMPLEX SENTENCE

A **complex sentence** includes *only one* main clause and *at least one* subordinate clause.

Examples: **Since she is, I am too.**

("Since she is, ..." – the subordinate clause; "...I am too." – the main clause)

I woke up because the rooster crowed in the early part of the day at the top of the hill by the barn.

("I woke up..." – the main clause; "...because the rooster crowed...," – the subordinate clause)

NO PERMISSION HAS BEEN GRANTED BY N&N PUBLISHING COMPANY, INC TO REPRODUCE ANY PART OF THIS BOOK BY ANY MECHANICAL, PHOTOGRAPHIC, OR ELECTRONIC PROCESS.

THE COMPOUND-COMPLEX SENTENCE

A **compound-complex sentence** includes *at least one* subordinate clause and *at least two* main clauses, the last *two* of which are joined by a coordinating conjunction preceded by a comma.

Examples: **Since she is, I am too, but neither of us is happy about the situation.**

("Since she is, ..." – the subordinate clause; "...I am too ...," – the 1st main clause; "...but neither ..." – the 2nd main clause)

Adelle awoke because the rooster crowed in the early part of the day at the top of the hill by the barn, and she was not able to sleep through any type of noise.

("Adelle awoke" – the 1st main clause; "because the rooster ... by the barn," – the subordinate clause clause; "...she was not able to sleep..." – the 2nd main clause)

SENTENCE TYPE PRACTICE

Here are several sentences for you to identify.

Directions: Read each sentence and on the line provided identify which type of sentence it is (simple, compound, complex, or compound-complex).

1.   In the early light, I could see the outline of the tree. _____

2.   Because it was such a large and majestic oak, my friend Flick and I used to play under it on hot days. _____

3.   We were young and had few responsibilities. _____

4.   Every summer's day we played there until dark, and I really miss those days. _____

5.   If I get a good education, I'll be able to really change my life, and then I can be on my own. _____

RECOGNIZING THE PREDICATE – VERBS

A predicate is the main action of a group of words or a way of existing. If I am a bit shaky about finding a predicate, I can try these four rules (on the next page):

NO PERMISSION HAS BEEN GRANTED BY N&N PUBLISHING COMPANY, INC TO REPRODUCE ANY PART OF THIS BOOK BY ANY MECHANICAL, PHOTOGRAPHIC, OR ELECTRONIC PROCESS.

1. I look for a part of the verb "to be" or an action word. Parts of the verb "to be" include am, is, are, was, were, will be, has, or have been.

   Examples: **He <u>was</u> here.** (part of the verb "to be")

   I often <u>rushed</u> through dinner in order to go out later. (action word)

2. I make sure that there is no "to" in front of the suspected predicate.

   Example: **On the way to his house to see him, I <u>fell</u> down.** (Because there is a "to" in front of "his" and "see," I know that the predicate here is "fell" and not "his" or "see.")

3. In my mind, I try putting one of the following pronouns in front of the suspected predicate; if it sounds right with just one of these pronouns, I go on to the next step.

   Pronouns to try: I, you, he, she, it, we, they

   Example: **The last day of school <u>seems</u> so near now.** ("It seems" sounded right to me, and so I go to step 4.)

4. I make sure that somebody or something in the sentence is performing the action of the predicate.

   Example: **The last day of school seems so near now.** ("It seems" sounded correct and there is something in that group of words that "seems" [the <u>day</u> seems]. Good, I have found my predicate.)

My teacher showed me another approach to finding the predicate that often helps me. She said to try putting a time word such as "tomorrow" or "yesterday" in front of the sentence. The sentence takes on a new meaning, and the word (or words) that changes will be the predicate.

   Example: **He represented his client in court. <u>Tomorrow</u> he will represent his client in court.** ("Represented" had to change, so that must be the predicate, and it is.)

NO PERMISSION HAS BEEN GRANTED BY N&N PUBLISHING COMPANY, INC TO REPRODUCE ANY PART OF THIS BOOK BY ANY MECHANICAL, PHOTOGRAPHIC, OR ELECTRONIC PROCESS.

Now that I know how to find the predicate, finding the subject of a group of words is easy because a subject is the "do-er" of the predicate.

Example: **<u>Menemsha</u> creates beautiful patterns of knots.** (Following the rules for finding the predicate and the suggestion to put a time word in front of the sentence, I discover that "creates" is the predicate. The proper noun "Menemsha" is the do-er of "creates," so "Menemsha" is the <u>subject</u>.)

SUBJECT AND PREDICATE PRACTICE 1

Here is an exercise that I will use to practice picking out the subject and predicate of a group of words.

Directions: <u>Underline</u> the <u>subject</u> and put parentheses ( ) around the (predicate) in each of the following sentences.

1. Adelle threw the ball to Molly.

2. Kim questioned the victim about the accident.

3. After losing the game, Fyodor left the park and decided not to go out that night.

4. Wishing won't make things happen.

5. The seriousness of the injury became clear later that day.

6. Her desire to become famous motivated her to try very hard.

7. At the first sight of him, they began to run away.

8. To begin with, the teacher never seemed to notice him.

9. This test requires focus and practice on the part of the student.

10. Madeline and Bill carefully approached the growling dog.

Knowing how to find predicates and subjects helps me to focus on the key ideas in a piece of reading. On the next page is another paragraph for me to read.

NO PERMISSION HAS BEEN GRANTED BY N&N PUBLISHING COMPANY, INC TO REPRODUCE ANY PART OF THIS BOOK BY ANY MECHANICAL, PHOTOGRAPHIC, OR ELECTRONIC PROCESS.

SUBJECT AND PREDICATE PRACTICE 2

Directions: Underline the subjects and put parentheses ( ) around the (predicates) in this paragraph. Notice the nouns and pronouns which are similar and are repeated: voter, he, voting booth, voting, and voting booth.

The new voter nervously approached the voting booth. He had used the machine in social studies class, but that was not the real thing. This time he would be pulling the levers, and the electronic systems would record his vote. As the curtain of the booth closed behind him, he felt suddenly truly mature and very important. Unlike smoking or other pseudo-adult activities, voting was something that no child could do. The voting booth really did separate the men from the boys and the women from the girls.

RECOGNIZING A TOPIC SENTENCE

As reading skills, finding the subjects and predicates and noticing repeat nouns and pronouns give me clues as to the focus of the paragraph. What is the control sentence or the **topic sentence** of the paragraph above? Since the paragraph is about how the first time voter is nervous but feels special because voting is a truly adult activity, the topic sentence is the last sentence.

When I read, repeated nouns and my knowledge of predicates and subjects helps me to unlock the key idea in a paragraph. When I write, this knowledge helps me communicate clearly. Since any essay is built paragraph by paragraph, I now have a key to help me unlock the meaning of the entire essay, paragraph by paragraph.

As I read paragraph by paragraph, it is good for me to get into the habit of jotting down the key idea next to the paragraph or at least underlining the topic sentence. This will help me to answer questions about the paragraph.

NO PERMISSION HAS BEEN GRANTED BY N&N PUBLISHING COMPANY, INC TO REPRODUCE ANY PART OF THIS BOOK BY ANY MECHANICAL, PHOTOGRAPHIC, OR ELECTRONIC PROCESS.

TOPIC SENTENCE PRACTICE

Directions: Underline the topic sentence in the paragraph. Make a list of repeated nouns and pronouns and repeated subjects and their predicates to focus on the basic idea and choose the correct topic sentence.

In order to pick the best people for political offices, it is necessary for the voters to understand the issues and the candidates. Voters should read newspapers, magazines, and political brochures in order to inform themselves. In addition, the electorate, the people eligible to vote, should listen to debates on the radio and television. Further, voters should attend meetings at which candidates appear. At those meetings, voters should attempt to question candidates about important issues.

REVIEW OF PUNCTUATION CONVENTIONS

My writing responses on the test will be scored on writing mechanics (or conventions) such as punctuation, grammar, and spelling (see rubric page 119). I must use punctuation marks as road signs to help others understand what I mean when I write.

MARKS AT THE END OF A SENTENCE

• **Periods** (.) must be placed at the end of all declarative sentences (e.g., *We are going on an ocean voyage.*), and they should be placed at the end of those imperative sentences that do not express strong emotion (e.g., *Please keep moving in the hallway.*). Periods must also be used with most abbreviations.

• **Exclamation points** (!) are used to end sentences that show emotion (e.g., *The Titanic is sinking!*).

• **Question marks** (?) end interrogative sentences (direct questions) (e.g., *Were there any survivors?*).

NO PERMISSION HAS BEEN GRANTED BY N&N PUBLISHING COMPANY, INC TO REPRODUCE ANY PART OF THIS BOOK BY ANY MECHANICAL, PHOTOGRAPHIC, OR ELECTRONIC PROCESS.

COMMA (,) RULES

Learning to use commas properly makes a world of difference in writing. The two sentences below use the same words, but I can see that the placement of commas changes the meaning.

Examples: **Let's forget Bill and still be friends.**

Let's forget, Bill, and still be friends.

It is important for me to review some very basic comma rules starting with the rule that makes such a difference in the example sentences.

1. Use a comma to set off the name of the audience to which the sentence is directed.

    Example: **Let's forget, Bill, and still be friends.** (Here we are speaking to Bill, not about him. The use of the commas before and after the word ", Bill," allows the reader to know that Bill is the audience to whom the sentence is directed.)

2. Use a comma after every item in a series (three or more items) except for the last.

    Example: **We ate popcorn, peanuts, apples, and chocolate.**

3. Use a comma after an introductory prepositional or participle phrase. A preposition is one of those fairly short words which ties a noun or a pronoun to the rest of the sentence in what is called a prepositional phrase (example: in the morning). A participle is a verb ending in -ing or -ed (examples: excited by the cheering or exciting the crowd).

    Examples: **In the morning, I was awakened by the rooster.** (introductory prepositional phrase)

    Excited by the rooster's crowing, the old man removed his shoes and danced. (introductory participle phrase)

    Exciting the crowd, the rooster seemed to imitate popular rock stars. (introductory participle phrase)

NO PERMISSION HAS BEEN GRANTED BY N&N PUBLISHING COMPANY, INC TO REPRODUCE ANY PART OF THIS BOOK BY ANY MECHANICAL, PHOTOGRAPHIC, OR ELECTRONIC PROCESS.

4. Use a comma to separate the tag of a quotation from the rest of the sentence. The tag is the "she said" part.

    Examples: **"I am," he said, "the best baseball player in the city."**

                        He said, "I am the best baseball player in the city."

                        "I am the best baseball player in the city," he said.

5. Use a comma before the coordinating conjunction used to join the two independent clauses in a compound or compound-complex sentence.

    Examples: **Elias swims, and Marisa does too.** (Two main clauses joined by ", and" in a compound sentence.)

                        Elias swims, and Marisa does too when she has the time. (Two main clauses joined by ", and" in a compound-complex sentence.)

6. Use a comma following an introductory dependent clause.

    Example: **Because T.J. likes to fish, Sundeep bought a rod for T.J. as a birthday present.** ("Because T.J. likes to fish" is an introductory subordinate clause.)

7. Use a comma to set off interruptions in the sentence. These interrupters might be words, phrases, or entire subordinate clauses.

    Examples: **Mr. Kim, principal, attended the meeting of the PTA last night.**

                        Janelle, the captain of the squad, led the cheer.

                        My sister, who is younger than I, lives next to Mr. Smith.

NO PERMISSION HAS BEEN GRANTED BY N&N PUBLISHING COMPANY, INC TO REPRODUCE ANY PART OF THIS BOOK BY ANY MECHANICAL, PHOTOGRAPHIC, OR ELECTRONIC PROCESS.

USING THE APOSTROPHE (')

The **apostrophe sign** (') is used to indicate three things in a sentence: (1) the possessive case, (2) plurals of numbers, letters, and abbreviations, and (3) the omission of a letter or letters from a word.

Examples: **John's dog Spot caught the Frisbee in the air. Then, Spot ran away with the Frisbee. Now the Frisbee is Spot's.** (singular possessive)

At the party, the girls' coats were hung neatly in the closet, but the boys' coats were thrown in a pile. (plural possessive)

Examples: **In the late 1800's, steam engines were used by the railroads.** (plurals of numbers)

I received all A's on my last report card. (plurals of letters)

My mother is a psychiatrist, and my father is a surgeon. I'm lucky to have two M.D.'s in my family. (plurals of abbreviations)

Example: **The contraction form of the word cannot is can't.** (omission of letters)

CAPITALIZATION

- Capitalize the first word of every sentence, line of poetry, and quotation.

- Capitalize all proper nouns (names of persons, persons' titles, specific places, titles of books, plays, motion pictures, and news media).

Example: **During a job interview, Mr. Arkwright, Manager of Smythe's Department Store, asked Jordan, "Do you read the *Wall Street Journal?*"**

PUNCTUATION CONVENTIONS PRACTICE

Here are several sentences for you to practice your punctuation skills.

Directions: For each of the following sentences, (1) underline each word that should have been Capitalized and (2) place the proper punctuation in each of the blank boxes.

NO PERMISSION HAS BEEN GRANTED BY N&N PUBLISHING COMPANY, INC TO REPRODUCE ANY PART OF THIS BOOK BY ANY MECHANICAL, PHOTOGRAPHIC, OR ELECTRONIC PROCESS.

1. since tyler arrived early☐ he needs to ask you to move your car so that he can leave and pick up his brother☐

2. i want to ask her to the concert☐ but i don't have the money right now because I haven't been paid yet☐

3. yes☐ jung shoo can play football well☐ but he also is an excellent student☐

4. after putting the dog inside☐ moe forgot to close the gate☐ and the dog ran right after him☐

5. kosh and koreen agreed with me and voted for my candidate☐ but ali chose to vote for his friend☐

6. what is wrong with yolanda today☐

7. wow☐ that was an exciting ride☐

8. mr☐ mccarthy☐ the conductor☐ said☐ "i don't recall the girls☐ names☐ but i know they were wearing central high jackets☐"

9. if you can☐t trust your own judgement☐ what☐s the point of running a business☐

10. oh no you don☐t☐ you keep your hands off that pie☐ it is jenny☐s entry for the chenango county fair☐

NO PERMISSION HAS BEEN GRANTED BY N&N PUBLISHING COMPANY, INC TO REPRODUCE ANY PART OF THIS BOOK BY ANY MECHANICAL, PHOTOGRAPHIC, OR ELECTRONIC PROCESS.

NO PERMISSION HAS BEEN GRANTED BY N&N PUBLISHING COMPANY, INC TO REPRODUCE ANY PART OF THIS BOOK BY ANY MECHANICAL, PHOTOGRAPHIC, OR ELECTRONIC PROCESS.

LISTENING

REVIEW OF LISTENING SKILLS

Listening requires the use of very specific and important skills. To do well on the test, I need to practice using these skills. This requires another person to read to me, so that I may listen. Because I may not always have someone to help me, I practice my listening skills in class. I can do this by actually listening to my teacher and to those students who take part in class discussions.

I have tried this practice during class, and it works. But to remember what I will need to know to write my answers on the test, I must take notes. My notes will be the basis for my writing. When my teacher speaks, I try to ask myself these questions:

- To whom is the writer speaking? (audience)

- What is the writer's topic? (task)

- Where or what is the writer's setting? (place)

- What are the writer's facts? Facts are observations without interpretation. Facts are those things which are able to be proven:

    sights
    sounds
    tastes
    tactile impressions (things one can feel)
    smells

- What are the writer's opinions? Opinions are confident beliefs which have not been clearly proven.

    For example, how I feel about a person or a character is an opinion until I offer proof in the form of facts. Just because I have a strong opinion about something, doesn't make that thing clearly true to anyone other than me.

- When did the event under discussion occur? (fact)
  Why did the event take place? (facts and/or opinions)
  What were the immediate causes? (facts and/or opinions)
  What were the underlying causes? (facts and/or opinions)

- How did this event affect others or other things? (opinion)

NO PERMISSION HAS BEEN GRANTED BY N&N PUBLISHING COMPANY, INC TO REPRODUCE ANY PART OF THIS BOOK BY ANY MECHANICAL, PHOTOGRAPHIC, OR ELECTRONIC PROCESS.

The beauty of this practice exercise is that I can use it for every class and every day. Not only will I be better prepared for this test, but also I will probably do better in each class as a result of this practice. I will also learn to take my notes this way as I listen to lectures and discussions in class.

LISTENING PRACTICE

Directions: The listening selection for this practice question is in the back of this book (page 113). **Do not look at it yourself**. Have someone read it to you twice. Listen carefully to the passage the first time but do not take notes. As you listen to the passage the second time, take notes. (Before beginning this practice, review the note-taking advice above.)

Use your notes to answer the question on page 37.

"Women's Ice Hockey"

•   Who is the audience?

_____

_____

_____

•   What is the topic?

_____

_____

NO PERMISSION HAS BEEN GRANTED BY N&N PUBLISHING COMPANY, INC TO REPRODUCE ANY PART OF THIS BOOK BY ANY MECHANICAL, PHOTOGRAPHIC, OR ELECTRONIC PROCESS.

- What are the facts? (people, events, places, dates, times)

  _____

  _____

  _____

  _____

  _____

  _____

  _____

- What are the opinions?

  _____

  _____

  _____

  _____

- What are the causes and effects?

  _____

  _____

  _____

  _____

Question

Why would the author of the essay feel that women's ice hockey is now a genuine sport? Use information from the essay to support your answer.

  _____

  _____

  _____

  _____

  _____

  _____

  _____

  _____

NO PERMISSION HAS BEEN GRANTED BY N&N PUBLISHING COMPANY, INC TO REPRODUCE ANY PART OF THIS BOOK BY ANY MECHANICAL, PHOTOGRAPHIC, OR ELECTRONIC PROCESS.

NO PERMISSION HAS BEEN GRANTED BY N&N PUBLISHING COMPANY, INC TO REPRODUCE ANY PART OF THIS BOOK BY ANY MECHANICAL, PHOTOGRAPHIC, OR ELECTRONIC PROCESS.

8TH GRADE PRACTICE TEST NUMBER ONE

(WITH STEP-BY-STEP INSTRUCTIONS)

SESSION 1

Time for Session 1 of the test: 90 minutes.

Directions: Read the following article, story, and narrative essay and answer questions about what you have read. You are encouraged to look back at the reading itself as often as you like.

READING PASSAGE 1

Directions: Read "A Little Help for the Candidate from the NYS Board of Elections" and then answer Questions 1-8.

A Little Help for the Candidate from the NYS Board of Elections

If a citizen has ever complained about the quality of candidates running for office in your local or state elections, that citizen might consider running for office himself or herself. "Running for Elective Office in New York State" is a publication of the New York State Board of Elections. Reading this document is a very good first step for the novice (beginner) who is considering running for office for the first time. The publication is designed to aid those people who are preparing to run for public office or party position.

NO PERMISSION HAS BEEN GRANTED BY N&N PUBLISHING COMPANY, INC TO REPRODUCE ANY PART OF THIS BOOK BY ANY MECHANICAL, PHOTOGRAPHIC, OR ELECTRONIC PROCESS.

The general information offered on petitions[1] indicates that this Board of Elections document provides a general guide to a potential candidate, but the specific regulations of which a candidate must be aware are listed in Article 6 and Article 15 of the Election Law. If a person really wants to run for office, that individual should obtain a copy of that law and study it carefully. That potential candidate should also contact the New York State Board of Elections located at Swan Street in Albany or his/her county board of elections. The latter can be located through a phone book or by contacting the NYS Board of Elections. The candidate needs to do his/her homework on the requirements for running for office so that his/her opponent will not be able to say that he or she has violated the election laws of New York State or his or her county.

The process of running for office involves many steps. First, a candidate must have petitions signed by registered voters. The number of names necessary for each candidate is proportionate to the number of people who will be represented by the candidate. For example, in 1998, to run for a statewide office such as governor, candidates needed to have petitions signed by at least 15,000 people – at least 100 or 5% of whom (whichever would be less) had to come from 16 different congressional districts. However, if a candidate had run for an assembly district in 1998, only 500 signatures would have been necessary. These petitions must be precise and have very specific information, so the candidate must carefully follow the election law regarding petitions.

After a candidate has the petitions signed by the required number of voters, the candidate must file the petitions with the state. Where the petition is filed depends on the office for which the candidate is running. The booklet indicates where the congres-

> "Political parties may nominate a candidate who is not an enrolled member of the political party. Such candidates must file a certificate of authorization, signed and acknowledged by the presiding officer and the secretary of the meeting at which such authorization is given."
> –*Running for Elective Office in New York State*, March 1998

NO PERMISSION HAS BEEN GRANTED BY N&N PUBLISHING COMPANY, INC TO REPRODUCE ANY PART OF THIS BOOK BY ANY MECHANICAL, PHOTOGRAPHIC, OR ELECTRONIC PROCESS.

sional, senate, and assembly district petitions for public office should be filed.

The booklet also contains information concerning contributions and receipt limitations. A candidate should know about who may contribute to his/her campaign and how much each contributor is allowed to give. Since contributors include individuals, corporations, other candidates' political committees, unincorporated union or trade organizations, Political Action Committees (PACs), or any groups such as leagues or associations, it is imperative that candidates be aware of the rules regarding contributions and contributors.

So when a person considers running for public office, he/she should also remember to pick up the "Running for Elective Office in New York State" publication. This guide will help by reminding the candidate about which laws to check, which people to contact, and which process to follow.

---

1 petitions - A formal written document requesting a right or benefit from a person or group in authority.

Big 8 Advice

You should read this article once and then read the questions. As you read the article the second time, keep the questions in mind. Read with a pencil in hand so that you can underline the topic sentences of each paragraph. That underlining will make answering the "main idea" or "author's purpose in writing this" questions much easier to answer. Check your topic sentence choices with those in this book. Remember that the topic sentence is the control sentence of the paragraph and one good way to find it is to see which nouns and pronouns are repeated. That will help you see what the main idea of the paragraph is.

Directions: Answer Questions 1-8 based on the reading above.

1   What is the main idea of this article?
   A   to describe the process of electing candidates in the United States
   B   to discuss the campaign finance issues
   C   to encourage all candidates to read the NYS Board of Elections publication
   D   to prevent fraud among federal employees

NO PERMISSION HAS BEEN GRANTED BY N&N PUBLISHING COMPANY, INC TO REPRODUCE ANY PART OF THIS BOOK BY ANY MECHANICAL, PHOTOGRAPHIC, OR ELECTRONIC PROCESS.

2 Candidates who are nominated by political parties of which they are not members must

   A not run
   B become members of the party which nominates them
   C not file any petitions
   D file a certificate of authorization

3 A candidate needs to follow the election laws of New York State so that s/he will not

   A be jailed
   B be publicly challenged by his or her opponents
   C have to redo all of the steps of the nomination process
   D be contacted by federal authorities

4 The text indicates that 15,000 people were required to sign petitions for state wide offices in 1998 because that number

   A has always been the same since the start of this century
   B will change according to the population of New York State
   C is just a suggestion
   D is also used for county elections

5 A PAC is a

   A Congressional district
   B Senatorial district
   C Board of Election supervisor
   D Political Action Committee

6 The only type of New York State voter who may sign any petition for public office or political party is one who is a

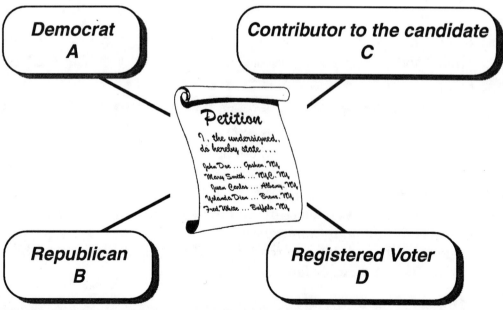

Democrat
A

Contributor to the candidate
C

Petition

I, the undersigned, do hereby state …

John Doe … Goshen, NY
Mary Smith … NYC, NY
Juan Carlos … Albany, NY
Yolanda Dion … Bronx, NY
Fred White … Buffalo, NY

Republican
B

Registered Voter
D

NO PERMISSION HAS BEEN GRANTED BY N&N PUBLISHING COMPANY, INC TO REPRODUCE ANY PART OF THIS BOOK BY ANY MECHANICAL, PHOTOGRAPHIC, OR ELECTRONIC PROCESS.

7 "Running for Elective Office in New York State" was published by the
   A League of Women Voters
   B county and state census bureaus
   C New York State Regents
   D New York State Board of Elections

8 If there are problems with the petitions, the person held responsible is
   A the Board of Elections supervisor
   B the head of the political party to which the candidate belongs
   C the contributors to the candidate's election finances
   D the candidate

Now I will work on Session I, Reading Passage 2.

READING PASSAGE 2

Big 8 Advice

This reading is a personal essay. It is much less formal in organization than the first type of essay. Read this essay and search for answers to the questions: Who? What? When? Where? Why? and How? Underline the answers to these questions as you come across them in your first reading. Then read the short answer questions. On your rereading of the essay after you have read the questions, look for the answers to those specific questions.

Directions: Read this story about how an immigrant's name was changed. Then answer Questions 9-18.

How My Family Became Green

My grandmother tells the story of how her father became green shortly after his arrival in the United States from Italy. It was a very long time ago, but to this day my mother and father and three sisters and I have green in our background because of what happened to my great-grandfather.

My great-grandfather had saved his money and taken steerage[1] passage to the United States around the end of the 1900s. His cousins lived in New Jersey, very

---

1   Steerage - The section of a passenger ship, originally near the rudder, providing the cheapest passenger accommodations.

NO PERMISSION HAS BEEN GRANTED BY N&N PUBLISHING COMPANY, INC TO REPRODUCE ANY PART OF THIS BOOK BY ANY MECHANICAL, PHOTOGRAPHIC, OR ELECTRONIC PROCESS.

close to New York City, so he knew that when he got to this country, he would have somewhere to stay while he was finding a job and getting settled. My great-grandfather's name was Giuseppe Verdi, just like the famous composer who wrote that great opera, *La Traviata* in 1853. My great-grandfather was a smart young man who studied a little English before he came here and started night school English classes almost as soon as he arrived.

Because my great-grandfather Giuseppe was in good health and was a strong and willing worker, he got a job on the Erie Lackawana Railroad. It was a hard job, and Giuseppe worked long hours, but he believed in the American dream – that if one worked hard, one could make a good life in this new country. So he went to work for the railroad the month after he got off the boat from Europe.

The man who hired Giuseppe was kind but had difficulty hearing well. Also, my great-granfather spoke with a very noticeable accent. So, when Giuseppe told the boss his name for the fifth time and the boss could not understand it, my great-grandfather said, "My name is really very simple. Giuseppe means "Joe" in English and Verdi means "Green." My name is "Giuseppe Verdi." The boss hired my great-grandfather and he started work that same day.

Pay day was two weeks later. Giuseppe was very excited the day that he was supposed to receive his first pay envelope. He wanted to pay rent to his cousins and buy them a nice gift for letting him stay with them. Giuseppe also wanted to send some money home to his mother in Italy because times were hard for his family back home.

When my great-grandfather received his pay, he was upset. The amount of money was correct, but the name on the envelope was wrong. It read "Joe Green." Giuseppe went to the boss to try to have the error corrected.

The boss just smiled as my great-grandfather respectfully tried to explain the problem with his name. After Guiseppe finished explaining, the boss shook his hand and said, "Not to worry, Joe. That money is all yours; you worked hard for it, Joe Green, and nobody, not even this Giuseppe Verdi fellow, is entitled to take it from you. Welcome to the United States."

NO PERMISSION HAS BEEN GRANTED BY N&N PUBLISHING COMPANY, INC TO REPRODUCE ANY PART OF THIS BOOK BY ANY MECHANICAL, PHOTOGRAPHIC, OR ELECTRONIC PROCESS.

My great-grandfather worked that job under the name of Joe Green for three years until his boss retired. After that, my great-grandfather was successful in having the new boss change the records to "Giuseppe Verdi," but neither my great-grandfather nor the rest of our family has ever forgotten how, for a while at least, my family became green.

Directions: Answer Questions #9-18 based on the reading above.

9 The author's grandmother was
  A   an immigrant from Italy
  B   the daughter of Giuseppe Verdi
  C   a young Irish woman
  D   born after the narrator

10 One reason why Giuseppe Verdi was able to immigrate was that he
  A   paid for his plane ticket early
  B   was related to the boss at the train yards
  C   had relatives in New Jersey
  D   was in poor health

11 The basic idea of this story is about how
  A   sometimes immigrants had their names changed by their employers
  B   Italian is a difficult language
  C   Green is a common name in Italy
  D   many greedy people took advantage of the immigrants

12 One reason that Giuseppe Verdi immigrated to the United States was that he
  A   came from a family of wealthy investors in Italy
  B   was running away from his family
  C   was an orphan
  D   believed in the American dream

13 The boss smiled at Giuseppe when Giuseppe became upset about the pay envelope because the boss
  A   was prejudiced against immigrants
  B   didn't understand why Giuseppe was upset and was trying to be reassuring
  C   thought that Giuseppe was quitting
  D   was going to retire soon

14 Where did Giuseppe study English?
  A   only in America   **C**   in the train yard
  B   in Italy and America   **D**   at his cousin's house

NO PERMISSION HAS BEEN GRANTED BY N&N PUBLISHING COMPANY, INC TO REPRODUCE ANY PART OF THIS BOOK BY ANY MECHANICAL, PHOTOGRAPHIC, OR ELECTRONIC PROCESS.

15 Giuseppe didn't scream at his boss and demand the name on the pay envelope be changed because

    A   Giuseppe was respectful

    B   the boss was a violent man

    C   Giuseppe spoke no English

    D   the boss spoke no Italian

16 When the text says, "Giuseppe worked under the name of Joe Green," it means

    A   Giuseppe worked for Joe Green

    B   Joe Green lived above Giuseppe

    C   the name of the railroad boss was Joe Green

    D   Giuseppe used the alias, false name, of Joe Green

17 *La Traviata* is mentioned in this essay because the narrator's

    A   great-grandfather wrote it

    B   great-grandfather hummed it all of the time

    C   great-grandfather had the same name as the author of that music

    D   boss loved that opera

18 The boss says "not even this Giuseppe Verdi fellow is entitled to take it from you." "Entitled" means

    A   prevented

    B   willing

    C   allowed

    D   wanting

READING & WRITING

STOP

FOR INFORMATION & UNDERSTANDING

READING PASSAGE 3

Directions: Here is the third of the three pieces of reading. Read this essay which was written by a graduating high school senior in response to choosing the most important words she had ever heard. Then do Questions 19 through 25.

Big 8 Advice

> Remember that titles are important. Also remember that you need to read with a pencil in hand underlining the topic sentences of each paragraph. As you underline these sentences, keep the question words: who, what, where, why, when, and how in mind. This will greatly aid your ability to focus as you read.

NO PERMISSION HAS BEEN GRANTED BY N&N PUBLISHING COMPANY, INC TO REPRODUCE ANY PART OF THIS BOOK BY ANY MECHANICAL, PHOTOGRAPHIC, OR ELECTRONIC PROCESS.

The Lorax and Me

I am about to leave high school and start a college course of study which will enable me to become a biology researcher. If I work hard and am lucky, I will spend much of my life studying the life on our planet and helping all species to survive together. So, when I chose the words which were most important to me, I wanted to connect those words with my future and my past. I look forward to being a biological researcher because of words my mother spoke but didn't actually make up herself. The most important words in my life were words from the Dr. Seuss book, *The Lorax*.

I was six when my mother first read the book to me. I had always loved all the Dr. Seuss books, but as the story of the Lorax and his relationship with nature unfolded, I felt an interest I had never before felt in any other subject. It seemed that the book about how nature can so easily be destroyed by the greed of people who were more interested in making money or having more and more things was being told just to me.

I looked at the pictures of the trees being chopped down and the birds getting sick in the polluted environment, and I knew that I had to find a way to help.

A few years, later the tragic oil spill on the Alaskan shoreline reminded me of how fragile our environment is. Dr. Seuss was still right. The television pictures of dead birds and sea animals left permanent images in my mind. For a social studies project, I wrote a report, "The Exxon Valdez Oil Spill," and drew pictures to illustrate it. I got an A, and I found my career. I was going to be a scientist.

From that day to this, I've taken many different kinds of science courses, and I have learned a great deal. I know that there is much more to learn, and I look forward to it because I see a point to learning what I can about all the living things on this planet.

I learned years ago from Dr. Seuss and his Lorax that I am the one who can make a difference and save this planet. The Lorax told me so, and he told you that too.

NO PERMISSION HAS BEEN GRANTED BY N&N PUBLISHING COMPANY, INC TO REPRODUCE ANY PART OF THIS BOOK BY ANY MECHANICAL, PHOTOGRAPHIC, OR ELECTRONIC PROCESS.

Directions: Answer Questions 19-25 based on the reading above.

19 The most important words the senior claims to have heard were from

   A   her science teacher   **C**   Dr. Seuss

   B   her father   **D**   the junior science fair

20 Which quotation from the essay best indicates why Dr. Seuss is so important to the senior today?

   A   "From that day to this, I've taken many different kinds of science courses, and I have learned a great deal."

   B   "I got an A, and I found my career."

   C   "The Lorax told me so, and he told you that too."

   D   "So, when I chose the words which are most important to me, I wanted to connect my future with my past."

21 The event in the senior's life that helped her to see that she might be able to help the environment as the Lorax had asked her was her

   A   graduation from high school

   B   good relationship with her mother

   C   fondness for animals

   D   getting an A on her social studies report

22 The first time that the author had *The Lorax* read to her was significant because

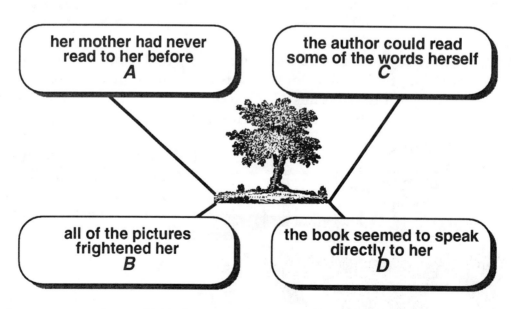

her mother had never read to her before
A

the author could read some of the words herself
C

all of the pictures frightened her
B

the book seemed to speak directly to her
D

23 The author seems to be realistic because she

   A   tells us her name

   B   knows she has a lot more to learn

   C   never wrote to the Lorax

   D   is from a single parent home

NO PERMISSION HAS BEEN GRANTED BY N&N PUBLISHING COMPANY, INC TO REPRODUCE ANY PART OF THIS BOOK BY ANY MECHANICAL, PHOTOGRAPHIC, OR ELECTRONIC PROCESS.

24 When the author says, "I see a point to learning what I can about all the living things on this planet," she means that she

    A sees a connection between her studies in biology and her desire to do biological research in the future

    B likes to take tests

    C enjoys getting good grades

    D likes science fiction

25 The text says that "nature can be destroyed by the greed of people." What is the meaning of greed?

    A the quality of being kind

    B a desire to possess more than one needs

    C morally wrong

    D slow to learn

**End of Reading Passages for Session 1.
Go on to Session 1 – The Listening Passages**

SESSION 1 (CONTINUED)

LISTENING PASSAGE 1

Directions: This is the listening and writing part of the first session. First you must listen to two essays: "A Man Like Me" and "A Thank You Note." Then answer some questions to show how well you understood what was read.

    The essays will be read twice. On the first reading, just listen. On the second reading, take notes. You can use the notes you take on the second reading to answer the questions about the readings.

    Here are two vocabulary words you may need to review before we begin:

    Abolitionist = a person dedicated to ending the practice of slavery

    eloquent = able to speak and /or write well

NO PERMISSION HAS BEEN GRANTED BY N&N PUBLISHING COMPANY, INC TO REPRODUCE ANY PART OF THIS BOOK BY ANY MECHANICAL, PHOTOGRAPHIC, OR ELECTRONIC PROCESS.

After hearing "A Man Like Me" read the first time, you must take notes on what you just heard. Make a chart (below) on your page and fill in the information that you can remember from the first listening experience.

Title of Listening Passage:		
Who?	**What?**	**Where?**
Why?	**When?**	**How?**

Then before hearing the passage read again, read the questions that you must answer about this listening passage. Having read the questions, you now know what to listen for as you hear the passage read a second time.

During the second reading, add to the notes in your chart, filling in the gaps.

After the second reading of "A Man Like Me," prepare a second chart for the next listening passage, "A Thank You Note." Then listen to the second passage. As you listen, keep in mind what you know about the passage and see if anything about the passages is similar.

NO PERMISSION HAS BEEN GRANTED BY N&N PUBLISHING COMPANY, INC TO REPRODUCE ANY PART OF THIS BOOK BY ANY MECHANICAL, PHOTOGRAPHIC, OR ELECTRONIC PROCESS.

"A Man Like Me"
(passage found on page 114)

Important: This reading passage is found in the
             Appendix at the back of this book on
             page 114. **Do not look at it yourself**.
             You want someone to read it to you.
             However, before you go ahead with
             the question, read the Big 8 Advice to
             the left.

Frederick Douglass 1817-1895

LISTENING PASSAGE 2

A Thank You Note
(passage found on page 114)

Important: This reading passage is found in the Appendix at the back of this book
             on page 114. Again, **do not look at it yourself**. You want someone to
             read it to you.

             However, before you go ahead with the question, read the Big 8 Advice
             found on the next page.

NO PERMISSION HAS BEEN GRANTED BY N&N PUBLISHING COMPANY, INC TO REPRODUCE ANY PART OF THIS BOOK BY ANY MECHANICAL, PHOTOGRAPHIC, OR ELECTRONIC PROCESS.

After hearing "A Thank You Note" read, you need to take notes. Make a chart on your page and fill in the information that you can remember from the first listening experience.

Title of Listening Passage:		
Who?	**What?**	**Where?**
Why?	**When?**	**How?**

Now read the questions that you must answer about this listening passage. Having read them, you now know what to listen for as you hear the passage read again. Then fill in some more notes on your sheet.

As you listen, I keep in mind what you know about the first passage and see if anything about the passages is similar.

26 Use the graphic organizer chart at the top of the next page to indicate what the Thank You Note narrator and Frederick Douglass had in common.

NO PERMISSION HAS BEEN GRANTED BY N&N PUBLISHING COMPANY, INC TO REPRODUCE ANY PART OF THIS BOOK BY ANY MECHANICAL, PHOTOGRAPHIC, OR ELECTRONIC PROCESS.

26 Answer (chart)	
Narrator	**Frederick Douglass**

Big 8 Advice

Look at the graphic organizer chart that you just made. See what was important about Douglass based on shared experiences with the narrator. Use information from your notes to document your answer.

27   Why was Frederick Douglass such an important person to the narrator?

_____

_____

_____

_____

_____

_____

_____

_____

_____

_____

NO PERMISSION HAS BEEN GRANTED BY N&N PUBLISHING COMPANY, INC TO REPRODUCE ANY PART OF THIS BOOK BY ANY MECHANICAL, PHOTOGRAPHIC, OR ELECTRONIC PROCESS.

Big 8 Advice

Suggestion: Use some specifics from the essay to support your response.

Go back to your notes and see what the similarities and differences were between the two people. Make sure that your topic sentence begins by addressing the differences.

28   How is the life of the high school senior different from that of Frederick Douglass?

_____

_____

_____

_____

_____

_____

_____

_____

_____

_____

Big 8 Advice

You have completed the short response questions for Session 1 of the test. Now, you have the one extended response question left to do. Each extended response question begins with a planning page followed by the actual question and space to write your essay.

Before going on to extended response Question 29, read the Big 8 Advice on pages 58 through 60. It reviews essay writing skills, including sentence types and paragraph arrangement.

NO PERMISSION HAS BEEN GRANTED BY N&N PUBLISHING COMPANY, INC TO REPRODUCE ANY PART OF THIS BOOK BY ANY MECHANICAL, PHOTOGRAPHIC, OR ELECTRONIC PROCESS.

PAGE 54   ENGLISH – BIG 8 REVIEW (ENGLISH / LANGUAGE ARTS 8TH GRADE TEST) N&N©

PLANNING PAGE FOR TASK NUMBER 29 (The task is stated on the next page.)

Directions: You can use this page to plan your writing, but do not write your final copy here. Whatever you write on the planning page will not count toward your final grade. Write your final answer on the next page next to the number 29.

BIG 8 ADVICE FOLLOWS QUESTION

NO PERMISSION HAS BEEN GRANTED BY N&N PUBLISHING COMPANY, INC TO REPRODUCE ANY PART OF THIS BOOK BY ANY MECHANICAL, PHOTOGRAPHIC, OR ELECTRONIC PROCESS.

29 Discuss the experiences of Frederick Douglass and the high school senior.

In your discussion be sure to include
- a description of the experiences of both people
- a comparison of the types of experiences each has had
- how each individual has been affected by his experiences

- Check your writing for correct spelling, grammar, and punctuation.

Big 8 Advice

The icon here reminds you to check your writing for correct spelling, grammar, and punctuation. Remember that the test asks you to write about what you have heard. Your writing will NOT be scored based on your personal opinions.

_____
_____
_____
_____
_____
_____
_____
_____
_____
_____
_____
_____
_____
_____
_____
_____
_____
_____
_____

NO PERMISSION HAS BEEN GRANTED BY N&N PUBLISHING COMPANY, INC TO REPRODUCE ANY PART OF THIS BOOK BY ANY MECHANICAL, PHOTOGRAPHIC, OR ELECTRONIC PROCESS.

_____

_____

_____

_____

_____

_____

_____

_____

_____

_____

_____

_____

_____

_____

_____

_____

_____

_____

_____

_____

_____

_____

_____

_____

_____

_____

_____

_____

_____

End of Session 1

NO PERMISSION HAS BEEN GRANTED BY N&N PUBLISHING COMPANY, INC TO REPRODUCE ANY PART OF THIS BOOK BY ANY MECHANICAL, PHOTOGRAPHIC, OR ELECTRONIC PROCESS.

Remember that this part of the test asks you to write about what you have listened to. Your writing will NOT be scored on the basis of your personal opinions. It WILL be scored on:

- how clearly you organize and express your ideas
- how accurately and completely you answer the questions
- how well you support your ideas with examples
- how interesting and enjoyable your writing is
- how correctly you use grammar, spelling, punctuation, and paragraphs

This writing task requires some thought. You need to underline the command of the question, "Discuss the experiences of Frederick Douglass and the high school senior." The question practically gives you an outline to follow when it reminds you, "In your discussion, be sure to include ...". Each of the points about which you are reminded should be a paragraph. In addition, you will need an introduction and a conclusion.

If you follow the test question outline, you should be able to do a good job on this question. Take your facts from your notes and from your answers to Questions 26, 27, and 28 (they are part of the prewriting).

MOTIVATOR SENTENCE

In your introduction, mention the people you are discussing and indicate when each of them lived. If possible, Try to start with a sentence which grabs the reader's attention. This sentence is called a motivator sentence.

Example: Although two people were born more than one hundred years apart, it is still possible for them to have common experiences.

BRIDGE SENTENCE

Now you need a bridge sentence or bridge sentences which connect the motivator to the topic sentence of the entire piece of writing.

Example: Frederick Douglass, an Abolitionist, author, speaker, and runaway slave, lived in the eighteen hundreds, yet it is possible for him to have a strong connection to high school seniors living today. One such senior recently wrote about his debt to Mr. Douglass.

NO PERMISSION HAS BEEN GRANTED BY N&N PUBLISHING COMPANY, INC TO REPRODUCE ANY PART OF THIS BOOK BY ANY MECHANICAL, PHOTOGRAPHIC, OR ELECTRONIC PROCESS.

THESIS SENTENCE (TOPIC SENTENCE OF PARAGRAPH ONE)

The main topic sentence is called the thesis sentence. Be careful to do exactly what the question asked, so you must write a thesis sentence about the experiences of Frederick Douglass and the high school senior.

Example: Both Frederick Douglass and a current high school senior used their experiences to try to make the world a better place.

To finish your introduction paragraph, see what the question wants you to cover first. It tells you to give a description of the experiences of both people. The combined examples above would result in this first paragraph:

Example: Although two people were born more than one hundred years apart, it is still possible to have common experiences. Frederick Douglass, an Abolitionist, author, speaker, and runaway slave, lived in the eighteen hundreds, yet it is possible for him to have a strong connection to high school seniors living today. One such senior recently wrote about his debt to Mr. Douglass. Both Frederick Douglass and a current high school senior shared experiences with learning.

TOPIC SENTENCE OF PARAGRAPH TWO

Make sure that the topic sentence of your second paragraph refers to the descriptions of the experiences of both people.

Example: Both Frederick Douglass and a current successful high school senior have had interesting experiences.

Now fill in the specifics from your earlier notes on the listening sections.

Example: Frederick Douglass was a slave in Maryland in the first half of the nineteenth century. When he was a slave, it was illegal for him to learn to read and write, but Douglass risked great punishment and taught himself to read and write. He ran away from slavery and went North where he did some speaking for the Abolitionist movement. The high school senior who wrote the essay is a soccer star who is preparing for college next year.

NO PERMISSION HAS BEEN GRANTED BY N&N PUBLISHING COMPANY, INC TO REPRODUCE ANY PART OF THIS BOOK BY ANY MECHANICAL, PHOTOGRAPHIC, OR ELECTRONIC PROCESS.

TOPIC SENTENCE OF PARAGRAPH THREE

The next point that the test wants you to concentrate on is a comparison of the types of experiences each of these people have had. Make sure that your topic sentence focuses on that.

Example: In many ways each of these people have had different experiences.

Now write the rest of the paragraph.

Example: Frederick Douglass underwent terrible hardships as a slave, and demonstrated tremendous bravery in risking his life to learn to read and write and later to escape from slavery. Douglass used his experiences as a way to encourage others who were against slavery. Douglass became a powerful and popular speaker in the North. The high school senior who wrote the essay has had successful experiences, but his success was not achieved by risking his life. The senior's success was the result of hard work, family and teacher support, and some fine role models.

TOPIC SENTENCE OF PARAGRAPH FOUR

The third area that the question wants you to focus on is how each individual was affected by his experiences. Be sure that the <u>topic sentence</u> for the fourth paragraph deals with this point.

Example: <u>Both Frederick Douglass and the senior who wrote the essay were positively affected by their experiences</u>. Frederick Douglass used his liberty to motivate others to fight the evil of slavery. The senior who wrote the essay used his success in soccer and school to continue on the road to education and to someday become a math teacher.

CONCLUSION PARAGRAPH

The last paragraph is the conclusion. You must restate the thesis statement, but use other words. Also, try to end with a memorable sentence.

Example: The escaped slave of the eighteen hundreds, Frederick Douglass, and the present day high school student used their experiences to try to help others. Good people, no matter what century they live in, use what life teaches them to try to make a positive difference in the world.

NO PERMISSION HAS BEEN GRANTED BY N&N PUBLISHING COMPANY, INC TO REPRODUCE ANY PART OF THIS BOOK BY ANY MECHANICAL, PHOTOGRAPHIC, OR ELECTRONIC PROCESS.

For this part of the test, you need to use both your reading skills and your writing skills. Use your question—word approach (who, what, where, why, when, how) to see similarities and differences between the two readings. You do not need to merely listen to these readings because you will have them in front of you, so you should underline any information that might answer one of the question words.

As you read this article, remember what you know about topic sentences and main ideas. Read with a pencil in hand. Keep in mind the question words: who, what, where, why, when, and how. Write notes on the article if you find answers to any of these questions.

PRACTICE TEST NUMBER ONE (CONTINUED)

SESSION 2

Time for this part of the test: 60 minutes.

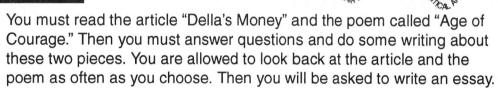

READING PASSAGE 1

Directions: You must read the article "Della's Money" and the poem called "Age of Courage." Then you must answer questions and do some writing about these two pieces. You are allowed to look back at the article and the poem as often as you choose. Then you will be asked to write an essay.

Della's Money

The second potato famine hit Ireland when Della Harte was young. Her family survived, but just barely. Della was the oldest of four, and together with her father and mother, she worked to keep the younger children fed and warm.

When Della was fifteen, her mother became pregnant with the youngest child. Three months before the baby was to be born, Della's father became ill and died. The family lived in Roscommon in the heart of Ireland, and the land they farmed was small and did not even

NO PERMISSION HAS BEEN GRANTED BY N&N PUBLISHING COMPANY, INC TO REPRODUCE ANY PART OF THIS BOOK BY ANY MECHANICAL, PHOTOGRAPHIC, OR ELECTRONIC PROCESS.

belong to them. It belonged to a landlord who expected that his rent be paid or the family would have to leave the land. Della's mother was desperate.

Her mother took what little money had been saved and instead of paying the landlord gave the money to Della. She walked Della to the Shannon River and said goodbye to her. A boat took Della down the Shannon to Limerick, where she made connections to go to Cork. From that city, she booked passage to America.

The trip across the ocean was terrifying to Della. She traveled steerage, in the lowest part of the ship. After weeks, the ship docked in New York and Della went through customs. She had been told in Cork that people would inspect the new arrivals and if she looked strong and healthy enough, she might be chosen to be

Mrs. Henry King and Della (1921). taken when the Kings – the lawyer and his wife who had employed Della –visited Della and her husband the year after they were married.

a maid for a family. She pinched her cheeks and stood tall as she walked through the last endless line at customs. When the customs official asked if she had anyone to vouch for her or to offer her employment, a gray haired man said that he would be offering Della a job working in the household of a dentist, Dr. Smithfield. Della smiled and left customs with the butler who brought her to the home of the dentist.

Della worked hard for the Smithfields. She worked in the kitchen for the first month, but soon became advanced enough to work upstairs making beds and cleaning. Della had told the Smithfields that she would need no part of her salary for herself since they were feeding her and giving her a uniform and a place to stay. She asked Dr. Smithfield to send her salary directly to her widowed mother in Roscommon.

NO PERMISSION HAS BEEN GRANTED BY N&N PUBLISHING COMPANY, INC TO REPRODUCE ANY PART OF THIS BOOK BY ANY MECHANICAL, PHOTOGRAPHIC, OR ELECTRONIC PROCESS.

After six months had passed, Della had become a trusted employee of the Smithfields and was given the task of buying some of the household goods. In all the time that Della had been with the Smithfields, she had never received any news from home. On her first shopping trip, Della asked for directions to the post office. There she asked for any mail addressed to Miss Della Harte, formerly of Roscommon, Ireland. Because she was so young and so anxious, the mail clerk promised to take some of his own time to look in the "dead letter" bins (addresses unknown). There he found three such letters. When she returned the next week to the post office, the mail clerk gave Della the letters from her mother.

As Della read the letters, she began to weep. In each of the increasingly intense letters, Della's mother first inquired, then demanded, then pleaded for the money which Della had promised to send home so that the family could pay the taxes and live. Della's mother had clearly received no money at all; in fact, she had no idea where Della was in that big city.

As she finished the last letter, Della sat on a bench and sobbed. A middle aged man stood in front of her and asked if he could be of help. Della did not know what to do, but there was no one else to ask for help, so she told the man her story. He smiled a kindly smile and took out a paper and wrote on it.

"Here," he said, "take this and go to this address. Show this to the butler. He will bring you to my wife. We are looking for someone to help her with the children, and you seem to be just the kind of girl we need. I will take care of Dr. Smithfield and make sure that he sends your mother the money she should have received, plus a little extra."

The kind gentleman was as good as his word. Mr. Henry King was a lawyer, and two months later Della received a grateful and apologetic letter from her mother saying that an extraordinary amount of money had just arrived and all would now be well with the family.

Della Harte worked for the lawyer and his family for thirteen years. During all of that time, she sent half of her salary home. When she was twenty-eight, she left Mr. King's service and married another immigrant. Together they raised seven children, one of whom became a lawyer, one a newspaper journalist, one a nurse, one a member of a religious order, one a decorated captain in World War II, one a postal worker, and one an accountant. Della never forgot Henry King's kindness, and she taught her children that it is the responsibility of each American to reach out to those in need of help.

NO PERMISSION HAS BEEN GRANTED BY N&N PUBLISHING COMPANY, INC TO REPRODUCE ANY PART OF THIS BOOK BY ANY MECHANICAL, PHOTOGRAPHIC, OR ELECTRONIC PROCESS.

In completing the graphic organizer chart in Question 30, think about how Della acted.

For Question 31, think about what Della did for her family, both in Ireland and in the United States. Begin the response with a topic sentence about what she did for her family showed how she felt about family.

Directions: Now you need to answer the questions about this reading.

30 Complete the chart with words or phrases that describe three qualities of Della and then list a fact or facts from the reading to use as evidence of this quality.

30 Answer (chart)	
Quality	**Supporting Detail**

31 How did Della Harte feel about family? Explain your answer using details from the article.

_____

_____

_____

_____

_____

_____

_____

_____

_____

NO PERMISSION HAS BEEN GRANTED BY N&N PUBLISHING COMPANY, INC TO REPRODUCE ANY PART OF THIS BOOK BY ANY MECHANICAL, PHOTOGRAPHIC, OR ELECTRONIC PROCESS.

Big 8 Advice

As you read the poem, "The Age of Courage," find the predicates and their subjects. That will enable you to keep straight what the poet is talking about even if the words are not all written in sentences on the same line. For example, the first predicate is *announce*, and the first subject is *calendars*. Also look for similarities between the poem and "Della's Money."

READING PASSAGE 2

The Age of Courage

Calendars announce occasions —
    Graduation, marriage, births,
All require time for aging,
    Years spent adding height and girth.

Can't a person under age
    Be mature and show some worth?
Surely youth must count for something—
    More than energy and mirth.

Leaving fondest friends and homes,
    Those youthful men and girlish women
Crossed a border or an ocean seeking here
    All they hoped and all they can.

Joining here the youth of natives
    And those who felt the slaver's greed,
All these young displayed great courage,
    Their wisdom, not their age, we heed.

Vocabulary:

fondest means dearest

mirth means joy

heed means to pay attention to

NO PERMISSION HAS BEEN GRANTED BY N&N PUBLISHING COMPANY, INC TO REPRODUCE ANY PART OF THIS BOOK BY ANY MECHANICAL, PHOTOGRAPHIC, OR ELECTRONIC PROCESS.

Big 8 Advice

To answer Question 32, first check the title of the poem. It is a good clue as to the main idea. Now check to see if a noun and its synonyms are repeated and what the predicates say about that noun. The noun "youth" and its synonym "young" shows up often. The poem asks if age is necessary for a person to be important, and then it answers that age is not important. However, it says wisdom and courage are important as we can see by the young immigrants, former slaves, and native Americans. Now you can respond. Be sure that your response begins with a topic sentence that tells what the main idea of the poem is.

32 What is the main idea of this poem? Use ideas from the poem to support your answer.

_____

_____

_____

_____

_____

_____

_____

_____

_____

_____

_____

Big 8 Advice

You have completed the short response questions for Session 2 of the test. Now, you have the last two extended response questions left. Each extended response question begins with a planning page, followed by the actual question and space to write your essay.

Before going on to extended response Question 33, read the Big 8 Advice on page 70. It reviews essay writing skills, including sentence types and paragraph arrangement.

NO PERMISSION HAS BEEN GRANTED BY N&N PUBLISHING COMPANY, INC TO REPRODUCE ANY PART OF THIS BOOK BY ANY MECHANICAL, PHOTOGRAPHIC, OR ELECTRONIC PROCESS.

PLANNING PAGE FOR TASK NUMBER 33 (The task is stated on the next page.)

Directions: You can use this page to plan your writing, but do not write your final copy here. Whatever you write on the planning page will not count toward your final grade. Write your final answer on the next page next to the number 33.

BIG **8** ADVICE
FOLLOWS
QUESTION

_____

_____

_____

_____

_____

_____

_____

_____

_____

_____

_____

_____

_____

_____

_____

_____

_____

_____

_____

_____

_____

_____

_____

NO PERMISSION HAS BEEN GRANTED BY N&N PUBLISHING COMPANY, INC TO REPRODUCE ANY PART OF THIS BOOK BY ANY MECHANICAL, PHOTOGRAPHIC, OR ELECTRONIC PROCESS.

33 Choose a line or some lines from the poem. Discuss the meaning of the part of the poem you have chosen and explain how this part of the poem applies to Della Harte. Use ideas from the poem and the article in your answer.

In your answer, be sure to include
- the line or lines you have selected from the poem
- an explanation of how your selection applies to Della Harte

- Check your writing for correct spelling, grammar, and punctuation.

Big 8 Advice

The icon here reminds you to check your writing for correct spelling, grammar, and punctuation. Remember that the test asks you to write about what you have heard. Your writing will NOT be scored based on your personal opinions.

_____
_____
_____
_____
_____
_____
_____
_____
_____
_____
_____
_____
_____
_____
_____
_____
_____
_____
_____

NO PERMISSION HAS BEEN GRANTED BY N&N PUBLISHING COMPANY, INC TO REPRODUCE ANY PART OF THIS BOOK BY ANY MECHANICAL, PHOTOGRAPHIC, OR ELECTRONIC PROCESS.

NO PERMISSION HAS BEEN GRANTED BY N&N PUBLISHING COMPANY, INC TO REPRODUCE ANY PART OF THIS BOOK BY ANY MECHANICAL, PHOTOGRAPHIC, OR ELECTRONIC PROCESS.

Question 33 provides you with an outline with which to answer it. Using that two point bulleted (•) outline, refer to your responses to the other questions about the article and poem (Questions 30-32) and come up with the details for your response.

First, underline what Question 33 wants you to do. Choose a line or lines from the poem and then discuss the meaning of that line or those lines. Then explain how that part of the poem applies to what you read about Della Harte.

Make this a multi-paragraph response. The first paragraph will be your introduction. The second paragraph will be the first bulleted (•) instruction to include the line or lines and explain them. The third paragraph will be the second bulleted (•) instruction to explain how this part of the poem applies to Della Harte. The last paragraph will be the conclusion.

I. Introduction
   A. Name the poem and the article
   B. Quote line or lines from the poem
   C. Say how these lines remind you of Della
II. Paragraph Two: Explain the meaning of the line or lines you chose
III. Paragraph Three: Explain how the line or lines reminds you of Della Harte
IV. Conclusion
   A. Restate tour thesis that the lines remind you of Della Harte
   B. End with a conclusion sentence which is memorable

Now, follow this outline and write your response on the lined section of the booklet where the final copy is to be written.

Be sure to pay attention to the icon of the pencil and paper which reminds you that especially on this part of the test you must check your writing for correct spelling, grammar, and punctuation.

Now you are ready to write the last essay of the test. As usual, you are given a planning page on which you may do all of your prewriting, but you must be sure to put the final copy on the lined page where it belongs.

Before you begin, check the Big 8 Advice on page 75.

NO PERMISSION HAS BEEN GRANTED BY N&N PUBLISHING COMPANY, INC TO REPRODUCE ANY PART OF THIS BOOK BY ANY MECHANICAL, PHOTOGRAPHIC, OR ELECTRONIC PROCESS.

PLANNING PAGE FOR TASK NUMBER 34 (The task is stated on the next page.)

Directions: You can use this page to plan your writing, but do not write your final copy here. Whatever you write on the planning page will not count toward your final grade. Write your final answer on the next page next to the number 34.

BIG 8 ADVICE FOLLOWS QUESTION

_____

_____

_____

_____

_____

_____

_____

_____

_____

_____

_____

_____

_____

_____

_____

_____

_____

_____

_____

_____

_____

_____

_____

_____

NO PERMISSION HAS BEEN GRANTED BY N&N PUBLISHING COMPANY, INC TO REPRODUCE ANY PART OF THIS BOOK BY ANY MECHANICAL, PHOTOGRAPHIC, OR ELECTRONIC PROCESS.

34 Write an essay about a person from history or someone whom you know who has demonstrated great courage.

In your essay be sure to include
- who the person is
- what he or she did to demonstrate courage
- the challenges he or she has faced
- how the challenges were overcome
- an introduction, a body, and a conclusion

Big 8 Advice

 The icon here reminds you to check your writing for correct spelling, grammar, and punctuation. Remember that the test asks you to write about what you have heard. Your writing will NOT be scored based on your personal opinions.

- Check your writing for correct spelling, grammar, and punctuation.

_____

_____

_____

_____

_____

_____

_____

_____

_____

_____

_____

_____

_____

_____

_____

_____

NO PERMISSION HAS BEEN GRANTED BY N&N PUBLISHING COMPANY, INC TO REPRODUCE ANY PART OF THIS BOOK BY ANY MECHANICAL, PHOTOGRAPHIC, OR ELECTRONIC PROCESS.

NO PERMISSION HAS BEEN GRANTED BY N&N PUBLISHING COMPANY, INC TO REPRODUCE ANY PART OF THIS BOOK BY ANY MECHANICAL, PHOTOGRAPHIC, OR ELECTRONIC PROCESS.

_____

_____

_____

_____

_____

_____

_____

_____

_____

_____

_____

_____

_____

_____

_____

_____

_____

_____

_____

_____

_____

_____

_____

_____

_____

_____

_____

This is the end of Practice Test One.

NO PERMISSION HAS BEEN GRANTED BY N&N PUBLISHING COMPANY, INC TO REPRODUCE ANY PART OF THIS BOOK BY ANY MECHANICAL, PHOTOGRAPHIC, OR ELECTRONIC PROCESS.

Read Question 34 and underline what the question asks you to do. Then check the bulleted (•) parts of the question because they will provide you with the outline that you will use for your answer.

Using the underlined command of the question and the bulleted reminders, assemble your outline for this response. Write about someone you know because it is easier for you to remember the details.

Since the bulleted reminders are so specific, do not use each as a paragraph source, but combine them:

I   Introduction
    A. Name the person
    B. Tell what he or she did to demonstrate courage
II. Discuss the challenges he/she faced and the courage shown
    A. Detail the problems
    B. Detail how he or she demonstrated courage
III. Conclusion
    A   Restate the thesis using other words
    B. Write a memorable last sentence

Now write your essay:

Now try a second practice test. Remember all that you reviewed in the first test and apply that knowledge to this second practice experience. This time though, try to keep track of your time. Your goal should be to complete the reading comprehension multiple choice section of the exam in forty-five minutes.

NO PERMISSION HAS BEEN GRANTED BY N&N PUBLISHING COMPANY, INC TO REPRODUCE ANY PART OF THIS BOOK BY ANY MECHANICAL, PHOTOGRAPHIC, OR ELECTRONIC PROCESS.

NO PERMISSION HAS BEEN GRANTED BY N&N PUBLISHING COMPANY, INC TO REPRODUCE ANY PART OF THIS BOOK BY ANY MECHANICAL, PHOTOGRAPHIC, OR ELECTRONIC PROCESS.

8TH GRADE PRACTICE TEST NUMBER TWO
(WITH STEP-BY-STEP INSTRUCTIONS)

SESSION 1

Time for Session 1 of the test: 90 minutes.

Directions: Read the following article, story, and narrative essay and answer questions about what you have read. You are encouraged to look back at the reading itself as often as you like.

READING PASSAGE 1

Directions: Here is an article concerning jury duty in one county in New York State. Read "Every Citizen's Privilege" and then answer Questions 1-8.

Every Citizen's Privilege

When Americans think of the jury system, many think of the protection it provides the average citizen. To be judged by a jury of one's peers (equals) is to be permitted to have other average citizens weigh the evidence against the accused and then come to a fair and thoughtful decision among themselves. This is quite a privilege; in some countries only the judge makes a decision, or possibly there is no trial at all, just a judgment at the scene of the crime and immediate punishment. Yes, being judged by a jury of one's peers is a privilege, but being on a jury is also a privilege since the only way to ensure the right to a jury trial is for citizens to fulfill their obligations to serve on juries.

NO PERMISSION HAS BEEN GRANTED BY N&N PUBLISHING COMPANY, INC TO REPRODUCE ANY PART OF THIS BOOK BY ANY MECHANICAL, PHOTOGRAPHIC, OR ELECTRONIC PROCESS.

The pay for jury duty in this Hudson River county is now forty dollars per day.

Who gets to serve on a jury? Well, in one county along the Hudson River in New York State, the process of selecting jurors involves many steps. The first step is to assemble a list of eligible jurors and send each person on that list a form to fill out and return. An eligible juror is one who is at least eighteen years of age, is a citizen of the United States, has never been convicted of a felony, and is able to communicate in English.

The county assembles a jury pool from lists of driver's license holders, lists of registered voters, lists of taxpayers, lists of the unemployed, lists of people who receive welfare benefits, and lists of volunteers. Each of the people on these lists is sent a form to fill out and return. Then all of the information on the returned forms is fed into a computer program, and the result is a list called the jury pool.

The computer program randomly selects a pool of 450 to 600 people to summon as jurors for any given week of the year. A juror who serves on a county jury may not be called by the county more often than once every four years. The juror who is summoned is given a number and instructed to call on the Sunday evening prior to the week during which he/she is eligible to be called for a jury.

That Sunday evening the juror will hear by phone which numbers are expected to be present in the courthouse the following day. If a juror's number is not called, he or she is instructed to remain on one hour stand-by. This stand-by means that the juror will be called either at home or at work one hour before it is necessary for the juror to be present in the courthouse. This one hour stand-by was revolutionary.

NO PERMISSION HAS BEEN GRANTED BY N&N PUBLISHING COMPANY, INC TO REPRODUCE ANY PART OF THIS BOOK BY ANY MECHANICAL, PHOTOGRAPHIC, OR ELECTRONIC PROCESS.

It allowed many potential jurors to go to work. In the past, they would have been sitting in the courthouse waiting to see if they were needed for a trial.

The fate of the juror will vary. If the juror is not called to the courthouse by Friday of the week for which the juror was summoned, he or she still has fulfilled the jury duty obligation and need not be concerned with any more jury duty for that year. If the juror had been called to the courthouse but not picked for a jury, he or she would also be excused from further duty for that session. Those jurors picked for the jury would have to be present for the run of the trial which might take anywhere from one day to several months.

Although the hours are long and the pay is not high, jurors continue to serve with honesty and responsibility. These jurors do so because they realize that if they or someone whom they loved were on trial, the privilege of being judged by a jury of one's peers only works if good, decent, hard-working people agree to serve on juries.

Big 8 Advice

Underline all of the topic sentences after taking a careful look at the repeated noun and its synonyms and pronouns which take its place in each paragraph. Notice that paragraphs two, four, five, six, and seven all have the same repeated noun: juror. You know that each of these paragraphs is saying something about the juror, so look at the predicates to see what the particular message of each paragraph is. When you do this, you can easily identify the topic sentence.

Since you can devote only half the Session I time (45 minutes) to the short answer sections and the three articles to read, practice reading with a pencil in hand so that you can increase your reading speed and your accuracy at the same time. Now quickly read through the questions answering those about which you are perfectly sure. Answer the rest after your second reading of the article.

1 The author's main reason for writing this article is to
   A complain about the inconvenience of jury duty
   B describe how a juror gets picked for duty in one county in New York State
   C describe the New York State court system
   D fully discuss the one hour stand-by system

NO PERMISSION HAS BEEN GRANTED BY N&N PUBLISHING COMPANY, INC TO REPRODUCE ANY PART OF THIS BOOK BY ANY MECHANICAL, PHOTOGRAPHIC, OR ELECTRONIC PROCESS.

2 The pay of the juror in this New York State county is
    A equal to one day on his/her job
    B good for a job which requires no manual labor
    C changing every year
    D forty dollars a day

3 The jury system works in the United States because of
    A highly paid lawyers
    B judges who never have to campaign for the popular vote
    C good, decent jurors
    D the Constitution

4 Those jurors who are summoned but are not called to the court house are
    A summoned again the next month
    B on standby for a week to several months
    C not placed on any juries for that session of the summons
    D sick people and old people

5 Which list is used in creating the jury pool?

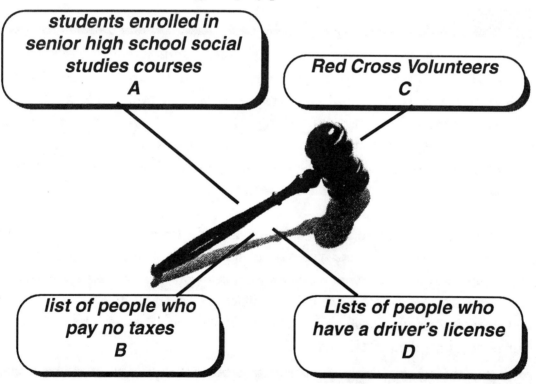

students enrolled in senior high school social studies courses **A**

Red Cross Volunteers **C**

list of people who pay no taxes **B**

Lists of people who have a driver's license **D**

6 The stand-by calling system is a great help especially to
    A mothers of young children
    B students in school
    C workers
    D those who are incapable of serving because of physical difficulty

NO PERMISSION HAS BEEN GRANTED BY N&N PUBLISHING COMPANY, INC TO REPRODUCE ANY PART OF THIS BOOK BY ANY MECHANICAL, PHOTOGRAPHIC, OR ELECTRONIC PROCESS.

7 In the New York State county being described, county trials are held in
  A large halls
  C Albany
  B fire stations
  D the courthouse

8 When the text states that the "stand-by system was revolutionary," it means
  A that one of the heroes of the American Revolution started this system
  B it is a new and different idea
  C it is an idea which conflicts with democracy
  D this idea dropped out after the American Revolution

Big 8 Advice

Now, without further delay, continue reading the next passage. As you read, look for answers to the questions
  • who?
  • what?
  • where?
  • why?
  • when?
  • how?

READING PASSAGE 2

Directions: Here is an article concerning the power of courtesy. Read "Courtesy Has Many Uses" and then answer Questions 9-18.

Courtesy Has Many Uses

Eduardo was my uncle. He came to this country when he was six. The area in which he lived had many ethnic neighborhoods, so Eduardo never thought it strange that people had different skin tones or haircuts or languages. When he was ten, Eduardo's family moved to an older neighborhood where most of the people looked and talked alike.

Most of Eduardo's neighbors were good Americans who respected every person and judged an individual by the way he or she behaved, not by skin tone, haircut, or language. Unfortunately, there were some exceptions, and two of them coached the soccer team that Eduardo had joined.

NO PERMISSION HAS BEEN GRANTED BY N&N PUBLISHING COMPANY, INC TO REPRODUCE ANY PART OF THIS BOOK BY ANY MECHANICAL, PHOTOGRAPHIC, OR ELECTRONIC PROCESS.

All season Eduardo had been on the bench. He played only when the team favorites were removed from the game for injuries. Eduardo had been a star player on his team in the old neighborhood, so he wondered why he was not playing much on the new team.

Eduardo practiced harder. He spent time practicing with several of the players on the team who had become his friends. His friends all told him to talk to the coaches because no one could imagine why Eduardo was not getting more game time.

When Eduardo approached the coaches, they listened with serious faces to his request to play more. Then, one at a time, they lectured him about being a team player. They told him that if he wanted to play, he would have to learn to allow them, as coaches, to use their good judgment and play those whom they trusted most to win. They told him that this was the American way and that, as one who was soon to become a naturalized citizen, Eduardo should understand the fairness of this system.

Eduardo listened to them and thanked them for their advice. He sat out all of the rest of the season, not even playing when other team members were injured. Despite that, Eduardo dressed in his uniform for each game, attended each practice, and waited for his fair chance to assist his team with the ability he knew he had.

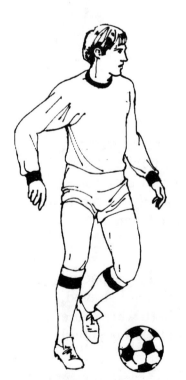

At the end of the season, the town honored all the spring sports players and their families. Eduardo's mother insisted that he wear his best sports jacket and slacks.

Admittedly, Eduardo had a little trouble recognizing himself in the mirror as the family left for the ceremony. As his aunt said, he "cleaned up nicely."

Eduardo, his mother, his aunt, and his teenage cousin Julia climbed onto the bleachers and sat down. They arrived early so that they got choice seats just in front of the coaches' section. The coaches in a long procession filed in and took their seats.

After the pledge of allegiance, Eduardo became aware of the voices behind him; they belonged to his soccer coaches. He was about to

NO PERMISSION HAS BEEN GRANTED BY N&N PUBLISHING COMPANY, INC TO REPRODUCE ANY PART OF THIS BOOK BY ANY MECHANICAL, PHOTOGRAPHIC, OR ELECTRONIC PROCESS.

turn around and say hello when the presentation of awards began and his mother gave him a look which let him know that this was not the time to socialize.

As the presentation of awards continued, Eduardo heard the distinctive coaches' voices behind him talking fairly loudly. To his surprise, the coaches seemed to have no problem with being rude during the ceremonies. And then, to Eduardo's great surprise, he heard the coaches discussing one of his friends, Con. The coach was ridiculing Con because of the way Con had lost his temper when the coach had yelled insults at Con during a game. The coach said, "Yeah, crazy Con. He's got no proof. It's his word against mine. Fat chance."

From there the remarks became more inappropriate as the coaches ridiculed almost everyone called up for an award. They would chuckle over one player's height, another's weight, and yet another's last name. They even made ethnic jokes about two of the players. Eduardo's face was burning.

He was incensed. How could these men be so hypocritical? How could they sit there in the special coaches' section and ridicule and belittle young people and then give lectures on being a good American? What should Eduardo do?

The look his mother gave him as he squirmed let him know what he should do. Eduardo remembered his father's saying: "Do not let those you dislike bring out things in yourself that you dislike. Meet stupidity, cruelty, and abuse of power with intelligence and courtesy. Use the most formal language you can to put fools in their places."

Just as the ceremony ended, Eduardo arose, turned, looked at the coaches, and said, "Ah, my coaches, I thought that was you. I heard you speaking during the presentations, and I thought that I must let you know that I recognize you."

And with that, Eduardo and his family filed out of the auditorium. It was only later that he found out that the videotape which his cousin Julia took of the ceremony had a remarkably sensitive audio unit which picked up all sorts of background noises.

NO PERMISSION HAS BEEN GRANTED BY N&N PUBLISHING COMPANY, INC TO REPRODUCE ANY PART OF THIS BOOK BY ANY MECHANICAL, PHOTOGRAPHIC, OR ELECTRONIC PROCESS.

9 This story is mostly about
   A mean coaches
   B soccer stars
   C the importance of a strong team
   D the value of using intelligence to fight ignorance and meanness

10 Eduardo attended the sports ceremony to
   A honor those receiving awards
   B get back at the coaches
   C receive an award
   D beg the coaches for more playing time

11 Eduardo had
   A no friends on the team
   B never played soccer before coming to the new neighborhood
   C a girlfriend named Julia
   D friends on the soccer team

12 When Eduardo spoke to the coaches about getting more playing time, they
   A lectured him on practicing good, American values
   B allowed him to play more
   C made fun of his name
   D made fun of his height

13 Eduardo was
   A tolerant of others' differences
   B used to being rude in front of his mother
   C never able to remember anything about his father
   D not good at soccer

14 When the coaches told Eduardo that he may not have more game time, he
   A thanked them for their advice   **C** never again went to practices
   B videotaped their response   **D** spit in their faces

15 The coaches did not see Eduardo because
   A they had been drinking
   B he was wearing a disguise
   C he was so short
   D he was all dressed up and was seated before they arrived

16 What is surprising about the end of the story?
   A Eduardo's mother praises the coaches.
   B The video camera has apparently picked up all that the coaches said during the ceremony.
   C Eduardo received the MVP Award for soccer.
   D The coaches are honored for their honesty and compassion.

NO PERMISSION HAS BEEN GRANTED BY N&N PUBLISHING COMPANY, INC TO REPRODUCE ANY PART OF THIS BOOK BY ANY MECHANICAL, PHOTOGRAPHIC, OR ELECTRONIC PROCESS.

17 When Eduardo's father told him that "the most formal language can put fools in their places," he meant
   A formal seating charts are important
   B use maps to show ignorant people how to go places
   C formal courtesy can be used to show people how ignorant and rude they are
   D fools are always lost

18 When the text states that "Eduardo was incensed," it means that
   A Eduardo was very angry
   B Eduardo was on fire
   C Eduardo smelled nice
   D Eduardo smoked

Big 8 Advice

Now read the last of the three short answer reading comprehension passages. Be sure to read carefully looking for topic ideas and answers to the questions: who, what, where, why, when, and how. Use a pencil to write on the test and underline key points.

READING PASSAGE 3

Directions: This was an address given to the senior class at the graduation exercises last year. Read this passage and then do Questions 19-25.

Education

One of the best teachers I ever had was a stern looking, slim old woman who wore her hair in the stylish blue tinted bun. As a kindergartner, I was truly terrified by all of the horror stories I had heard about her: she was nasty, she would spit at you if you couldn't tie your shoe laces (I couldn't, and this was before Velcro), and she consumed large quantities of lazy kindergartners for lunch but never gained any weight because she spent the rest of the day torturing the few remaining live students.

NO PERMISSION HAS BEEN GRANTED BY N&N PUBLISHING COMPANY, INC TO REPRODUCE ANY PART OF THIS BOOK BY ANY MECHANICAL, PHOTOGRAPHIC, OR ELECTRONIC PROCESS.

Somehow, through sheer luck and the ability not to inhale too deeply, I had survived all of September and October in her class. I had never yet actually seen her consume or torture anyone, and I made sure that my brother triple knotted my shoes, so I could not personally confirm the horror stories, but I knew that they were true. I just knew (and daily my older brother kept reminding me of the stories).

It was the big day of Halloween, and we were permitted to wear our costumes to school. My sixth grade brother had helped dress me as a hobo, a character wearing my brother's torn clothes and lots of charcoal beard and mustache. He had me wear a pair of wooden shoes. I believe they were actually souvenirs which my youngest uncle had brought home to us from one of his many jaunts. The shoes clunked as I walked, a feat which was not easy considering that the shoes were two sizes too big.

We went to the auditorium as soon as we got to school. Everyone lined up quickly, and then we began the costume walk. Suddenly, out of nowhere, my blue haired teacher yelled, "Who is making that terrible racket?" We all, even the sixth graders, stood still with panic.

Her eye perused my section of the line, and then I could feel her staring at my shoes. I prepared my soul for death.

Instead, however, she came up to me and bent down. "Can you really walk in those?" she asked.

"Well," I admitted, "it is pretty hard. They keep slipping off my feet."

"I'll tell you what," she said with a slight wink. "Why don't you take those off? I'll find you a pair of slippers or sneakers. I am afraid you will fall."

I went with her, to the relief of all of the other students. When we returned, the younger classes had just begun skipping around the outside aisle of the auditorium.

I stood absolutely still when she told me to join in the skipping. I couldn't do that.

I don't believe that I had ever skipped in my life.

NO PERMISSION HAS BEEN GRANTED BY N&N PUBLISHING COMPANY, INC TO REPRODUCE ANY PART OF THIS BOOK BY ANY MECHANICAL, PHOTOGRAPHIC, OR ELECTRONIC PROCESS.

Instead of yelling, this stately old blue haired lady took my hand and said, "Look, I'll show you how. It isn't too hard. Just follow me." Together we skipped around that whole auditorium.

She was a teacher. She generously gave of her dignity to show a small child how to skip. I will never forget her.

19 The title of the essay is "Education" because
    A it is about a school
    B the author is a teacher
    C the author remembers a lesson taught by a teacher
    D it takes place in a school auditorium

20 Which statement is exaggeration?
    A "I am afraid you will fall."
    B "I prepared my soul for death."
    C "She was a teacher."
    D "The shoes clunked as I walked."

21 The author is
    A a child now
    B unable to walk at all
    C a grown up
    D an old woman with blue hair

22 One source of the terrible stories about the kindergarten teacher was

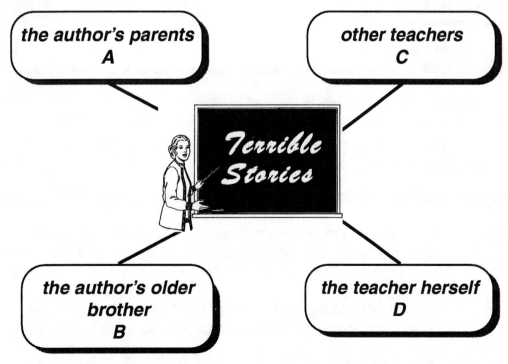

the author's parents
A

other teachers
C

the author's older brother
B

the teacher herself
D

NO PERMISSION HAS BEEN GRANTED BY N&N PUBLISHING COMPANY, INC TO REPRODUCE ANY PART OF THIS BOOK BY ANY MECHANICAL, PHOTOGRAPHIC, OR ELECTRONIC PROCESS.

23 The author asked her older brother to triple knot her shoes to
   A annoy the brother
   B please the parents
   C conceal her inability to tie shoes
   D appear important

24 The author probably wrote this story to
   A impress the older brother
   B indicate one of the qualities of a good teacher
   C please her parents
   D annoy the teacher

25 The shoes were probably souvenirs which "I believe my youngest uncle had brought home to us from one of his jaunts." A "jaunt" is a
   A factory   **C** business
   B trip   **D** jump

End of Session 1 Reading Passages.
Go on to the Session 1 Listening Passages.

SESSION 1 (CONTINUED)

LISTENING PASSAGE 1

Big 8 Advice

Here is the listening question. After the teacher has read the listening selections twice, the he or she will remind you that you have forty-five minutes to complete this section of the test. Remember that you may refer to any notes you have taken on the reading.

Directions: In this part of the test you will listen to two essays, "A New World, Another Planet" and "My Grandmother's Legacy," and then you will answer some questions to show how well you understood what was read.
You will listen to the essays twice. The first time you hear the essays, listen carefully but do not take notes. As you listen to the essays the

NO PERMISSION HAS BEEN GRANTED BY N&N PUBLISHING COMPANY, INC TO REPRODUCE ANY PART OF THIS BOOK BY ANY MECHANICAL, PHOTOGRAPHIC, OR ELECTRONIC PROCESS.

PAGE 88   *ENGLISH – BIG 8 REVIEW* (ENGLISH / LANGUAGE ARTS 8TH GRADE TEST) N&N©

second time, you may want to take notes. You may use these notes to answer the questions that follow.

Here are two phrases that you will need to know as you listen to the essays:

foot binding = a former practice in parts of China reserved for those women who would not be expected to perform household jobs. This was a method by which the feet of girls were broken and broken yet again and taped into small bandages. A woman with such feet was considered to have her beauty enhanced by the process of foot binding.

legacy = something handed down from an ancestor

"A New World, Another Planet" by Lee Wung
(passage found on page 115)

Big 8 Advice

If necessary, go back and review the use of this chart on page 50. Complete one for each listening question.

Title of Listening Passage:		
Who?	**What?**	**Where?**
Why?	**When?**	**How?**

NO PERMISSION HAS BEEN GRANTED BY N&N PUBLISHING COMPANY, INC TO REPRODUCE ANY PART OF THIS BOOK BY ANY MECHANICAL, PHOTOGRAPHIC, OR ELECTRONIC PROCESS.

LISTENING PASSAGE 2

Now listen to the words of Lee Wung's daughter, Dr. Su Wung.

"My Grandmother's Legacy" by Dr. Su Wung
(passage found on page 116)

Title of Listening Passage:

Who?	What?	Where?
Why?	**When?**	**How?**

NO PERMISSION HAS BEEN GRANTED BY N&N PUBLISHING COMPANY, INC TO REPRODUCE ANY PART OF THIS BOOK BY ANY MECHANICAL, PHOTOGRAPHIC, OR ELECTRONIC PROCESS.

26 Using specific details from the essay, complete the chart below to show what Lee Wung learned from his parents and from his experience after their death

Directions: Go back to your notes and use them to make this chart.

26 Answer (chart)	
Learned from Parents	**Learned from Experience (After Parents' Death)**

27 Why were the things that Lee Wung did after coming to America important to his future?

Big 8 Advice

Look at the graphic organizer chart you just made to see which things were important to Lee Wung's future after he came to America. Start your response with a topic sentence that focuses on the question asked. Then write a single paragraph response which uses details from the reading. Check your notes for help in this.

_____
_____
_____
_____
_____
_____
_____
_____
_____

NO PERMISSION HAS BEEN GRANTED BY N&N PUBLISHING COMPANY, INC TO REPRODUCE ANY PART OF THIS BOOK BY ANY MECHANICAL, PHOTOGRAPHIC, OR ELECTRONIC PROCESS.

Big 8 Advice

Be sure to start your response with a topic sentence that focuses on the question asked. Then write a single paragraph response using details from your notes to support your topic sentence. Go back to your notes to find these specifics.

28 How is Dr. Su Wung's life different from that of her grandmother?

_____

_____

_____

_____

_____

_____

_____

_____

_____

_____

_____

Big 8 Advice

You have completed the short response questions for Session 1 of the test. Now, you have the one extended response question left to do. Each extended response question begins with a planning page, followed by the actual question and space to write your essay.

Before going on to extended response Question 29, read the Big 8 Advice on pages 96 through 98. This advice reviews essay writing skills, including sentence types and paragraph arrangement.

NO PERMISSION HAS BEEN GRANTED BY N&N PUBLISHING COMPANY, INC TO REPRODUCE ANY PART OF THIS BOOK BY ANY MECHANICAL, PHOTOGRAPHIC, OR ELECTRONIC PROCESS.

PLANNING PAGE FOR TASK NUMBER 29 (The task is stated on the next page.)

Directions: You can use this page to plan your writing, but do not write your final copy here. Whatever you write on the planning page will not count toward your final grade. Write your final answer on the next page next to number 29.

BIG **8** ADVICE FOLLOWS QUESTION

_____

_____

_____

_____

_____

_____

_____

_____

_____

_____

_____

_____

_____

_____

_____

_____

_____

_____

_____

_____

_____

_____

_____

_____

_____

_____

_____

_____

NO PERMISSION HAS BEEN GRANTED BY N&N PUBLISHING COMPANY, INC TO REPRODUCE ANY PART OF THIS BOOK BY ANY MECHANICAL, PHOTOGRAPHIC, OR ELECTRONIC PROCESS.

29 Discuss the values of both Lee Wung and Dr. Su Wung.

In your discussion, be sure to include
- a discussion of the values of Lee Wung
- a discussion of the values of Dr. Su Wung

Your writing will be scored on:
- how clearly you organize and express your ideas
- how accurately and completely you answer the questions
- how well you support your ideas with examples
- how interesting and enjoyable your writing is
- how correctly you use grammar, spelling, punctuation, and paragraphs.

- Check your writing for correct spelling, grammar, and punctuation.

Big 8 Advice

The icon here reminds you to check your writing for correct spelling, grammar, and punctuation. Remember that the test asks you to write about what you have heard. Your writing will NOT be scored based on your personal opinions.

_____
_____
_____
_____
_____
_____
_____
_____
_____
_____
_____
_____
_____
_____

NO PERMISSION HAS BEEN GRANTED BY N&N PUBLISHING COMPANY, INC TO REPRODUCE ANY PART OF THIS BOOK BY ANY MECHANICAL, PHOTOGRAPHIC, OR ELECTRONIC PROCESS.

_____

_____

_____

_____

_____

_____

_____

_____

_____

_____

_____

_____

_____

_____

_____

_____

_____

_____

_____

_____

_____

_____

_____

_____

_____

_____

_____

End of Session 1. Session 2 begins on page 99.

NO PERMISSION HAS BEEN GRANTED BY N&N PUBLISHING COMPANY, INC TO REPRODUCE ANY PART OF THIS BOOK BY ANY MECHANICAL, PHOTOGRAPHIC, OR ELECTRONIC PROCESS.

Again, Question 29 asks you to write about what you have listened to. Your writing will NOT be scored on the basis of your personal opinions. It WILL be scored on:

- how clearly you organize and express your ideas
- how accurately and completely you answer the questions
- how well you support your ideas with examples
- how interesting and enjoyable your writing is
- how correctly you use grammar, spelling, punctuation, and para graphs

This piece of writing requires some thought. Underline the command of the question, "Discuss the values of both Lee Wung and Dr. Su Wung." The question gives you a bulleted (•) outline to follow when it reminds you of what to include in your answer. Each of the points about which you are reminded should be a paragraph. Then you also need an introduction and a conclusion.

If you follow that outline, you should be able to do a good job on this question. Take your facts from your notes and from Questions 26, 27, and 28.

MOTIVATOR SENTENCE

In your introduction, mention the people you are discussing and indicate their connections to each other. If possible, try to start with a sentence which grabs the reader's attention. This sentence is a motivator sentence.

Example: Lee Wung came from China and Dr. Su Wung, his daughter, was born in the United States, but both share more than their blood ties.

BRIDGE SENTENCE

Now you need a bridge sentence or bridge sentences which connect the motivator to the topic sentence of the entire piece of writing.

Example: The father and daughter share common values.

NO PERMISSION HAS BEEN GRANTED BY N&N PUBLISHING COMPANY, INC TO REPRODUCE ANY PART OF THIS BOOK BY ANY MECHANICAL, PHOTOGRAPHIC, OR ELECTRONIC PROCESS.

<u>THESIS SENTENCE</u>

Now you need to be careful to do exactly what the question asked, so you must write a thesis sentence about the values of Lee Wung and Dr. Su Wung.

Example: Lee Wung and Dr. Su Wung value independence, education, and family.

Now put these sentences together for your first paragraph.

Example: Lee Wung came from China and Dr. Su Wung, his daughter, was born in the United States, but both share more than their blood ties. The father and daughter share common values. Lee Wung and Dr. Su Ling value independence, education, and family.

TOPIC SENTENCE OF PARAGRAPH TWO:

At this point, see what the question bullets (•) remind you to discuss. The first bullet reminds you to discuss the values of Lee Wung. Fill in the specifics from your earlier notes on the listening section. Also, make sure that the topic sentence of your second paragraph refers to the values of Lee Wung.

Example: Lee Wung valued independence, education, and family.

Continue this paragraph with details from your listening notes.

Example: Mr. Wung valued independence because he knew that in America as an immigrant he had to rely on his own industry rather than his past if he were going to be successful. He also understood the value of education because he and his wife worked hard in their restaurant to make money and then switched jobs so that they could be with their only child and help her to get a good start to her education. Lee Wung sacrificed for his child by working long, hard hours and by devoting time to her education, so he valued family.

NO PERMISSION HAS BEEN GRANTED BY N&N PUBLISHING COMPANY, INC TO REPRODUCE ANY PART OF THIS BOOK BY ANY MECHANICAL, PHOTOGRAPHIC, OR ELECTRONIC PROCESS.

TOPIC SENTENCE OF PARAGRAPH THREE:

The next focal point that the second bullet (•) of the question addresses is the discussion of the values of Dr. Su Wung. Be sure that your topic sentence for paragraph three focuses on that topic.

Example: Dr. Su Wung also values independence, education, and family.

Now write the rest of the paragraph.

Example: Dr. Wung values independence and education because she says that she really appreciates her job. She also shows her value for these things, as well as for family, when she says how much she appreciates how her father and grandmother helped her to get a good education.

CONCLUSION PARAGRAPH

You have now done what the bulleted reminders in the question asked that you do, so you can write the conclusion paragraph. In this paragraph, you must restate the thesis using other words and try to end with a memorable conclusion sentence.

Example: Although fathers and daughters do not always agree, Mr. Lee Wung and his daughter, Dr. Su Wung, share common values. The fact that both these people share such fine values is a tribute to both of them.

Now check the spelling, grammar, and punctuation of your writing.

Also, check your time. The more you practice, the better you should be at all of these skills.

NO PERMISSION HAS BEEN GRANTED BY N&N PUBLISHING COMPANY, INC TO REPRODUCE ANY PART OF THIS BOOK BY ANY MECHANICAL, PHOTOGRAPHIC, OR ELECTRONIC PROCESS.

PRACTICE TEST NUMBER TWO (CONTINUED)

SESSION 2

Time for this part of the test: 60 minutes.

Directions: You must read the article, "Careening Career Change" by Diane Galante and "Dream Risks" by Enna Neoc. First you will answer questions and write about what you have read. You may look back at the passage and the poem as often as you like. Then you will be asked to write an essay.

Big 8 Advice

As you read , keep in mind all that you have practiced with topic words. topic sentences, and key question words (who, what, where, when, why, how). Use a pencil to underline key ideas as you read.

READING PASSAGE 1

Careening Career Change
by Diane Galante

What's he to lose?

"Careen" was one of the first English words Stanley Wyjorski learned when he immigrated to this country in the early 1900's. "Careen" means to swerve, rush headlong, or lurch while in motion. Stan learned this word because a careening coal car brought him to America.

Stanley Wyjorski was born in Poland in the late 1800's. His family was poor and worked a farm which couldn't support all eight of them, so when Stan, the oldest, was sixteen, he left home to go to the mines.

In Poland, as elsewhere in the 19th century, mine work was hard and dirty, and the hours were long. Men who worked the mines often died of diseases like "Black Lung" from breathing too much coal dust. Some died from mine explosions. And a few died as a result of careening coal cars.

The coal cars were fairly simple contraptions. They were big, metal dumpster-like containers which, when filled with coal, could weigh as

NO PERMISSION HAS BEEN GRANTED BY N&N PUBLISHING COMPANY, INC TO REPRODUCE ANY PART OF THIS BOOK BY ANY MECHANICAL, PHOTOGRAPHIC, OR ELECTRONIC PROCESS.

much as two hundred pounds. They were brought into the mines and filled with coal by the workers. The cars traveled on railroad type tracks.

The problem was that the mine tunnels were not level. They were as irregular as the rocks that had been blasted to make them. There were hills and curves on those hills. The coal cars remained stationary thanks only to a simple brake, and it sometimes did not hold. The tunnels were often just large enough for men, sometimes stooping to work. Often, there was not enough room for both the miners and the coal cars.

During his second month on the job, Stan heard the two men ahead of him in the torch-lit tunnel yell, "Car loose! Run!"

There was no place for Stan to run in time. He heard the car before he saw it. The tunnel was very narrow where Stan was working, and he was standing down hill in the tunnel from where the car had started to careen.

As he saw the car, he did the only thing possible. He threw himself face down between the tracks. He was poorly nourished and thin enough to fit. He later said that he would never forget the sound of the car passing over him. Stan said he prayed the whole time that the car

NO PERMISSION HAS BEEN GRANTED BY N&N PUBLISHING COMPANY, INC TO REPRODUCE ANY PART OF THIS BOOK BY ANY MECHANICAL, PHOTOGRAPHIC, OR ELECTRONIC PROCESS.

would not careen so much as to drop the heavy load of coal on top of him. He lived to tell his story.

The day after that happened, Stan reported to the mine office and said that he was quitting.

Stan decided that everything in life is dangerous, so he might as well follow a dream he had had since childhood and emigrate across the ocean to America. Stan said that one might as well take risks for a vision of a better tomorrow.

After two years, Stan found himself on a ship docking just off Manhattan Island. Stan made his dream come true each day after that through hard work and hope. Stan became a successful builder who married and raised three children: a nurse, a doctor, and a teacher. Stan always taught his children that risks are worthwhile if the dream is a good dream. Stan lived what he taught.

Big 8 Advice

Use your knowledge of the question words (who, what, where, why, when, and how) to help you to see what big decisions Mr. Wyjorski made and why he made them.

Directions: Now you need to answer the questions about this reading.

30 Complete the chart with words or phrases that describe three big decisions which Stanley Wyjorski made and tell why he made the decisions.

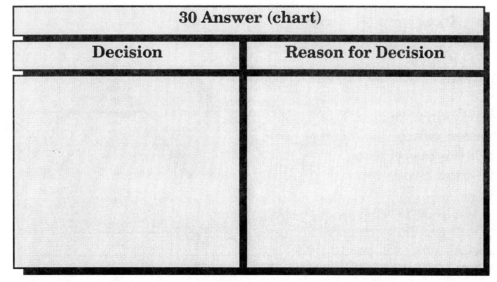

30 Answer (chart)	
Decision	**Reason for Decision**

NO PERMISSION HAS BEEN GRANTED BY N&N PUBLISHING COMPANY, INC TO REPRODUCE ANY PART OF THIS BOOK BY ANY MECHANICAL, PHOTOGRAPHIC, OR ELECTRONIC PROCESS.

31 How did Stanley Wyjorski feel about risks? Explain your answer using details from the article.

Big 8 Advice

In responding to this question, think about what happened to Stanley and how he viewed these incidents. Then begin with a topic sentence that speaks about the general attitude Stanley had about risks based on what he did and what he said.

_____

_____

_____

_____

_____

_____

_____

Big 8 Advice

Now read the following poem, "Dream Risks" by Enna Neoc and be prepared to answer a question about it. Remember to look for the predicates and their subjects in order to unlock the meaning of the poem. The title should also help to unlock the meaning. Also, remember that this test will ask you to find similarities and differences between the reading you just did, "Careening Careers" and this poem, "Dream Risks."

READING PASSAGE 2

"Dream Risks" by Enna Neoc

He chances pain or danger, loss –
With every breath, a risk he takes.
If only colds or fear of boss,
His daily grind has no retakes.

What's he to lose, he reasons sound,
In risking all to follow schemes:
Visions bright where hope abounds;
He tries becoming all he dreams.

NO PERMISSION HAS BEEN GRANTED BY N&N PUBLISHING COMPANY, INC TO REPRODUCE ANY PART OF THIS BOOK BY ANY MECHANICAL, PHOTOGRAPHIC, OR ELECTRONIC PROCESS.

So off he sets beyond his grasp
To reach the limits, grab the stars.
He chances ruin, unlocks the clasp –
And lives each day raising the bar.

Vocabulary:

abounds means having more than enough

"raising the bar" means increasing the performance level which is considered a challenge

Big 8 Advice

As you read the poem, keep track of the predicates and subjects. In the first stanza (a stanza is a division of a poem, similar to a paragraph in an essay) the first predicate is "chances" and the subject is "he." The next predicate is "takes" and the subject is "he"; the next predicate is "has" and the subject is "grind." Now respond to this question about the poem.

32 What is Enna Neoc saying about risks? Use ideas from the poem to support your answer (use lines on next page).

Big 8 Advice

In order to answer Question 32, first check the title of the poem. It is "Dream Risks" and that should be a good clue as to the main idea. Now check to see if a noun and its synonyms are repeated and what the predicate says about this repeated word. The noun "he" is repeated in stanza one. The predicates say that "he chances" and "he takes" (risks). In stanza two, "he" is repeated with the predicate " 's" (has) and "reasons." In stanza three "he" is repeated with the predicates "tries," "dreams," "sets," "chances," and "lives." The poem speaks of a person who takes risks daily and then decides that he will try to follow his dreams since he takes risks anyway, and his dreams will allow him to really live fully. Now you can respond. Be sure that your response begins with a topic sentence that tells what Enna Neoc is saying about risks.

NO PERMISSION HAS BEEN GRANTED BY N&N PUBLISHING COMPANY, INC TO REPRODUCE ANY PART OF THIS BOOK BY ANY MECHANICAL, PHOTOGRAPHIC, OR ELECTRONIC PROCESS.

(use lines for Task Number 32)_____

_____

_____

_____

_____

_____

_____

_____

_____

_____

_____

_____

_____

_____

_____

_____

_____

Big 8 Advice

You have completed the short response questions for Session 2 of the test. Now, you have the last two extended response questions left. Each extended response question begins with a planning page, followed by the actual question and space to write your essay.

Before going on to extended response Question 33, read the Big 8 Advice on page 108. The advice reviews essay writing skills, including sentence types and paragraph arrangement.

NO PERMISSION HAS BEEN GRANTED BY N&N PUBLISHING COMPANY, INC TO REPRODUCE ANY PART OF THIS BOOK BY ANY MECHANICAL, PHOTOGRAPHIC, OR ELECTRONIC PROCESS.

PLANNING PAGE FOR TASK NUMBER 33 (The task is stated on the next page.)

Directions: You can use this page to plan your writing, but do not write your final copy here. Whatever you write on the planning page will not count toward your final grade. Write your final answer on the next page next to the number 33.

BIG **8** ADVICE FOLLOWS QUESTION

_____

_____

_____

_____

_____

_____

_____

_____

_____

_____

_____

_____

_____

_____

_____

_____

_____

_____

_____

_____

_____

_____

_____

_____

_____

NO PERMISSION HAS BEEN GRANTED BY N&N PUBLISHING COMPANY, INC TO REPRODUCE ANY PART OF THIS BOOK BY ANY MECHANICAL, PHOTOGRAPHIC, OR ELECTRONIC PROCESS.

33 Choose a line or some lines from the poem. Discuss the meaning of the part of the poem you have chosen and explain how this part of the poem applies to Stan Wyjorski. Use ideas from the poem and the article in your answer.

In your answer be sure to include:
- the line or lines you have selected from the poem
- an explanation of how your selection applies to Stan Wyjorski

Big 8 Advice

The icon here reminds you to check your writing for correct spelling, grammar, and punctuation. Remember that the test asks you to write about what you have heard. Your writing will NOT be scored based on your personal opinions.

_____

_____

_____

_____

_____

_____

_____

_____

_____

_____

_____

_____

_____

_____

_____

_____

_____

_____

_____

NO PERMISSION HAS BEEN GRANTED BY N&N PUBLISHING COMPANY, INC TO REPRODUCE ANY PART OF THIS BOOK BY ANY MECHANICAL, PHOTOGRAPHIC, OR ELECTRONIC PROCESS.

NO PERMISSION HAS BEEN GRANTED BY N&N PUBLISHING COMPANY, INC TO REPRODUCE ANY PART OF THIS BOOK BY ANY MECHANICAL, PHOTOGRAPHIC, OR ELECTRONIC PROCESS.

Once again, this question has provided you with an outline with which to answer it. Using the two point bulleted (•) reminders, refer to your responses to the other questions about the article and poem (Questions 30-32) and come up with the details for your response.

First, underline what Question 33 wants you to do. First choose a line or lines from the poem, and then discuss the meaning of that line or those lines and explain how the line(s) apply to what you read about Stan Wyjorski. Make this a multi-paragraph response. The first paragraph will be your introduction. The second paragraph will be the first bulleted (•) instruction to include the line or lines from the poem and explain them. The third paragraph will be the second bulleted (•) instruction to explain how this part of the poem applies to Stan Wyjorski. The last paragraph will be your conclusion.

I. Introduction
   A. Name and author of poem and article
   B. Quote line or lines from poem
   C. Say how these lines remind you of Stan Wyjorski
II. Paragraph Two: explain the meaning of the line or lines from poem
III. Paragraph Three: explain how the line or lines reminds you of Stan
IV. Conclusion
   A. Restate your thesis that the line or lines remind you of Stan Wyjorski
   B. End with a conclusion sentence which is memorable

Now follow this outline and write your response on the lined section of the booklet where the final copy is to be written.

Be sure to pay attention to the picture of the pencil and paper which reminds you that, especially on this part of the test, you must check your writing for correct spelling, grammar, and punctuation.

NO PERMISSION HAS BEEN GRANTED BY N&N PUBLISHING COMPANY, INC TO REPRODUCE ANY PART OF THIS BOOK BY ANY MECHANICAL, PHOTOGRAPHIC, OR ELECTRONIC PROCESS.

PLANNING PAGE FOR TASK NUMBER 34 (The task is stated on the next page.)

Directions: You can use this page to plan your writing, but do not write your final copy here. Whatever you write on the planning page will not count toward your final grade. Write your final answer on the next page next to the number 34.

BIG **8** ADVICE FOLLOWS QUESTION

_____

_____

_____

_____

_____

_____

_____

_____

_____

_____

_____

_____

_____

_____

_____

_____

_____

_____

_____

_____

_____

_____

NO PERMISSION HAS BEEN GRANTED BY N&N PUBLISHING COMPANY, INC TO REPRODUCE ANY PART OF THIS BOOK BY ANY MECHANICAL, PHOTOGRAPHIC, OR ELECTRONIC PROCESS.

34 Write an essay about a person from history or someone whom you know who took some risks in order to pursue a dream.

In your essay be sure to include:
- who the person is
- what risks he or she took
- what the dream was that he or she pursued
- an introduction, a body, and a conclusion

Big 8 Advice

The icon here reminds you to check your writing for correct spelling, grammar, and punctuation. Remember that the test asks you to write about what you have heard. Your writing will NOT be scored based on your personal opinions.

_____
_____
_____
_____
_____
_____
_____
_____
_____
_____
_____
_____
_____
_____
_____
_____
_____
_____
_____
_____
_____

NO PERMISSION HAS BEEN GRANTED BY N&N PUBLISHING COMPANY, INC TO REPRODUCE ANY PART OF THIS BOOK BY ANY MECHANICAL, PHOTOGRAPHIC, OR ELECTRONIC PROCESS.

_____

_____

_____

_____

_____

_____

_____

_____

_____

_____

_____

_____

_____

_____

_____

_____

_____

_____

_____

_____

_____

_____

This is the end of Practice Test Two.

NO PERMISSION HAS BEEN GRANTED BY N&N PUBLISHING COMPANY, INC TO REPRODUCE ANY PART OF THIS BOOK BY ANY MECHANICAL, PHOTOGRAPHIC, OR ELECTRONIC PROCESS.

Now you are ready to write the last essay of the test, Question 34. As usual, you are given a planning page on which to do all of your prewriting, but be sure to put the final copy on the appropriate page.

Read Question 34 and underline what the question asks you to do. Then check the bulleted (•) parts of the question because they will provide you with the outline that you will use for your answer.

Using the underlined command of the question and the bulleted (•) reminders, assemble an outline for this response. Write about someone you know because it is easier for you to remember the details.

I. Introduction
   A. Name the person
   B. Tell his or her background

II. Discuss what risks he or she overcame

III. Discuss what dream he or she had

IV. Conclusion
   A. Restate the thesis using other words
   B. End with a memorable conclusion sentence

Now write your multi-paragraph essay.

NO PERMISSION HAS BEEN GRANTED BY N&N PUBLISHING COMPANY, INC TO REPRODUCE ANY PART OF THIS BOOK BY ANY MECHANICAL, PHOTOGRAPHIC, OR ELECTRONIC PROCESS.

APPENDICES

LISTENING PRACTICE 1 (PAGE 36)

Women's Ice Hockey

In 1998, women competed in ice hockey at the Winter Olympics for the first time. Four countries sent teams to the games in Nagano, Japan: Canada, China, Sweden, and the United States. The major reason why it took so long for this sport to be recognized by the Olympics has been the lack of financial support. In Canada, female players get low four hundred to eight hundred dollar monthly stipends (living allowances) from an Olympic support group, Sports Canada. Still, the sport is growing in popularity. USA Hockey reports the total number of women and girls now participating exceeds 23,000. Things may also change as corporations begin to sponsor players. Cammi Granato, the US team member who scored the first goal in Olympic women's hockey, signed an endorsement deal with Nike.

NO PERMISSION HAS BEEN GRANTED BY N&N PUBLISHING COMPANY, INC TO REPRODUCE ANY PART OF THIS BOOK BY ANY MECHANICAL, PHOTOGRAPHIC, OR ELECTRONIC PROCESS.

A Man Like Me

In Massachusetts in 1841, a group of Abolitionists held a convention to discuss the state of the country and its ties to the evil practice of slavery. Here a member of the convention comments on first meeting and hearing Mr. Frederick Douglass.

I met a man who has been to hell and lived to speak about it. I was fortunate to be asked by my good friend, Mr. William L. Garrison, to attend an anti-slavery convention in August of last year, 1841, in the town of New Bedford. There I was blessed by meeting and listening to the presentation of a newly escaped slave, Mr. Frederick Douglass.

As I listened to this eloquent man, I was struck by all that I remembered of my own experience before I bought my freedom from slavery in that same state, Maryland.

I, too, remembered the beatings of innocent women and children at the hands of their white owners. Although I did not learn to read and write until after buying my freedom and coming North, I do recall the threat of beatings or worse if any of the slaves dared to try to learn to read or write. Mr. Douglass, brave man that he is, risked this punishment and taught himself both reading and writing. His long exposure to books is surely evident in his brilliant speech. The entire hall of Abolitionists rose to their feet to applaud his story of his life as a slave.

A Thank You Note

I am seventeen and a senior in Centermain High School. I was recently awarded the MVP award for soccer, and I am proud of that, but my future is not going to be focused on sports. I intend to become a math teacher, and I just got accepted into one of the best state colleges, so I think that if I work hard, I will be successful.

There are lots of people I'd like to thank for this. My mom, of course, and all my family, as well as most of my teachers, have supported me and pushed me. But there are also people I need to thank whom I have never met.

NO PERMISSION HAS BEEN GRANTED BY N&N PUBLISHING COMPANY, INC TO REPRODUCE ANY PART OF THIS BOOK BY ANY MECHANICAL, PHOTOGRAPHIC, OR ELECTRONIC PROCESS.

I want to thank those heroic African American men like Frederick Douglass, who showed me what a privilege it is to be able to receive a public education. Douglass risked his life to learn to read and write, and he was so good at it that my English teacher has us analyze passages from Douglass to see how a really fine writer achieves power in his writing.

I didn't get this far alone, and I know that I will work to see that my children get even further.

LISTENING NUMBER 1, TEST 2 (PAGE 89)

"A New World, Another Planet" by Lee Wung

When I was a very young child, my parents told me how they lost the fortune which our family had for centuries. War came and our family was torn apart and scattered; our lands were lost, and our power and wealth disappeared with them. We had been a very important and a very well educated family. My father was a university man who traveled as far as Europe. My mother belonged to a very traditional family and even had her feet bound. When my parents were young, they expected that they would continue to be leaders of their community. The war changed all of that.

I was separated from my siblings after my parents were killed. I was lucky and found my way on a ship to England and, finally, to the United States. Once on American soil, I knew that my future depended not on my family's past but rather on my own industry. I worked long hours in a restaurant in Manhattan and saved my money. I bought my own little restaurant when I was thirty. There, my wife and I worked hard for eight years before our only child, Su, was born.

After Su's birth, I sold the restaurant, and we moved upstate. There, we both found jobs in an office during the day and kept our nights free so that between us, my wife and I could prepare Su for the wonderful education we planned for her. There was much sacrifice, but there was mostly great joy that in this country, with luck and with hard work, we could make a new life for our child. America gave us a new chance in a world which seemed to be on a different planet from the war-torn China we had known.

NO PERMISSION HAS BEEN GRANTED BY N&N PUBLISHING COMPANY, INC TO REPRODUCE ANY PART OF THIS BOOK BY ANY MECHANICAL, PHOTOGRAPHIC, OR ELECTRONIC PROCESS.

"My Grandmother's Legacy" by Dr. Su Wung

I am a doctor. I spend most of my time in laboratories looking for ways to rid mankind of terrible problems like AIDS and cancer. I love my job, and a day never goes by that I do not thank my grandmother for her legacy of courage and love.

My grandmother was an important woman in China when she was young. After she married, she and my grandfather lived productive lives as village leaders. Although my grandmother had been born into a very wealthy and traditional family – so traditional that they followed the practice of having Grandmother's feet bound – my grandmother was a very independent person. When her husband was killed in the war and her family began to lose its wealth and power, Grandmother called my father, her youngest son, to her. She pointed to her feet and said, "This was the legacy which my parents left me. I can not walk far nor run in advance of the troops. If you survive and grow to have a daughter, you must give her an education as grandma's legacy. Then she will be prepared for whatever life has to offer."

I never met my grandmother; I know her from my father's stories. She lived half a world away, but I love her and am grateful to her and to my father for obeying her last wish. I stand where I am today because my grandmother knew that a person must be prepared to stand alone under changing circumstances.

NO PERMISSION HAS BEEN GRANTED BY N&N PUBLISHING COMPANY, INC TO REPRODUCE ANY PART OF THIS BOOK BY ANY MECHANICAL, PHOTOGRAPHIC, OR ELECTRONIC PROCESS.

NO PERMISSION HAS BEEN GRANTED BY N&N PUBLISHING COMPANY, INC TO REPRODUCE ANY PART OF THIS BOOK BY ANY MECHANICAL, PHOTOGRAPHIC, OR ELECTRONIC PROCESS.

GRADE 8 ENGLISH SCORING RUBRIC - LISTENING / READING AND WRITING RUBRIC
Tasks 26, 27, 28, 29 (30, 31, 32, 33)

Quality	6 Responses at this level:	5 Responses at this level:	4 Responses at this level:	3 Responses at this level:	2 Responses at this level:	1 Responses at this level:
Meaning: the extent to which the response exhibits understanding and interpretation of the task and text(s)	*Taken as a whole:* – fulfill the requirements of the tasks – address the theme or key elements of the text – show an insightful interpretation of the text – make connections and demonstrate reflection	*Taken as a whole:* – demonstrate most of the characteristics of responses at the 6-point level, but they may show slightly less understanding, provide less elaboration, or lack the consistent quality of responses at the 6-point level.	*Taken as a whole:* – fulfill some requirements of the tasks – address some key elements of the text – show a predominantly literal interpretation of the text – make few connections	*Taken as a whole:* – are similar to responses at the 4-point level, but they may be weakly organized or sketchy, with ideas that are not supported by examples from the text. There may be a few minor inaccuracies, and the responses provide fewer details. The responses indicate that the student has read or listened to the entire text but experiences gaps in understanding the whole.	*Taken as a whole:* – fulfill some requirements of the tasks – address basic elements of the text – show little evidence that the student understood more than parts of the text – make few connections	*Taken as a whole:* – are more difficult to read and understand than responses at the 2-point level. The responses show evidence of comprehension of only parts of the text and may be repetitive focusing on minor details.
Development: the extent to which ideas are elaborated using specific and relevant evidence from the text(s)	*Taken as a whole:* – develop ideas fully with thorough elaboration – make effective use of relevant and accurate examples from the text		*Taken as a whole:* – may be brief, with little elaboration, but are sufficiently developed to answer the questions – provide some examples and details from the text		*Taken as a whole:* – may provide some text-based examples and details, but may contain some irrelevancies or inaccuracies	
Organization: the extent to which the response exhibits direction, shape, and coherence	*The extended response:* – establishes and maintains a clear focus – shows a logical, coherent sequence of ideas through the use of appropriate transitions or other devices		*The extended response:* – is generally focused, though may contain some irrelevant details or minor inaccuracies – shows a clear attempt at organization		*The extended response:* – may show an attempt to establish a focus – show little attempt at organization	
Language Use: the extent to which the response reveals an awareness of audience and purpose through effective use of words, sentence structure, and sentence variety	*The extended response:* – is fluent and easy to read, with vivid language and a sense of engagement or voice – is stylistically sophisticated, using varied sentence structure and challenging vocabulary		*The extended response:* – is readable, with some sense of engagement or voice – primarily uses simple sentences and basic vocabulary		*The extended response:* – uses minimal vocabulary – may indicate fragmented thoughts – is readable, with little sense of engagement or voice	

NO PERMISSION HAS BEEN GRANTED BY N&N PUBLISHING COMPANY, INC TO REPRODUCE ANY PART OF THIS BOOK BY ANY MECHANICAL, PHOTOGRAPHIC, OR ELECTRONIC PROCESS.

GRADE 8 ENGLISH SCORING RUBRIC - INDEPENDENT WRITING RUBRIC
TASK 32 (34)

Quality	3 Responses at this level:	2 Responses at this level:	1 Responses at this level:	0 Responses at this level:
Meaning: the extent to which the response exhibits understanding and interpretation of the task	– fulfill the requirements of the task – demonstrate insight make connections	– fulfill some requirements of the task – make some connections	– fulfill few requirements of the tasks – make few connections	– are completely incorrect, irrelevant or incoherent
Development: the extent to which ideas are elaborated using specific and relevant details and examples	– develop ideas fully with thorough elaboration – make effective use of relevant and accurate examples to support ideas	– may be brief, with little elaboration, but are sufficiently developed –provide some examples and details, but may exhibit difficulty in demonstrating how the examples related to or support the ideas	– may contain a few examples or details	
Organization: the extent to which the response exhibits direction, shape, and coherence	– establish and maintain a clear focus – show a logical, coherent sequence of ideas through the use of appropriate transitions or other devices	– are generally focused, though may contain some irrelevant details – show a clear attempt at organization	– may focus on minor details, or do not establish a focus – show little or no organization	
Language Use: the extent to which the response reveals an awareness of audience and purpose through effective use of words, sentence structure, and sentence variety	– are fluent and easy to read, with vivid language and a sense of engagement of voice – are stylistically sophisticated, using varied sentence structure and challenging vocabulary	– are readable, with some sense of engagement or voice – primarily use simple sentences and basic vocabulary	– are often repetitive, with little or no sense of engagement or voice – use minimal vocabulary – may indicate fragmented thoughts	

GRADE 8 ENGLISH SCORING RUBRIC - WRITING MECHANICS RUBRIC
Task 31, 32, 36 (29, 33, 34)

Quality	3 Responses at this level:	2 Responses at this level:	1 Responses at this level:	0 at this level:
Conventions: the extent to which the response exhibits conventional spelling, punctuation, paragraphing, capitalization, grammar, and usage	– The writing demonstrates control of the conventions of written English. There are few, if any, errors and none that interfere with comprehension. Grammar, syntax, capitalization, punctuation, and paragraphing are essentially correct. Any misspellings are minor or repetitive; they occur primarily when a student takes risks with sophisticated vocabulary.	– The writing demonstrates partial control of the conventions of English. It contains errors that may interfere somewhat with readability but do not substantially interfere with comprehension. There may be some errors of grammar, syntax, capitalization, punctuation, or spelling.	– The writing demonstrates minimal control of the conventions of written English. There may be many errors of grammar, syntax, capitalization, punctuation, and spelling that interfere with readability and comprehension.	– The writing demonstrates a lack of control of the conventions of written English. The errors make the writing incomprehensible

NO PERMISSION HAS BEEN GRANTED BY N&N PUBLISHING COMPANY, INC TO REPRODUCE ANY PART OF THIS BOOK BY ANY MECHANICAL, PHOTOGRAPHIC, OR ELECTRONIC PROCESS.

NO PERMISSION HAS BEEN GRANTED BY N&N PUBLISHING COMPANY, INC TO REPRODUCE ANY PART OF THIS BOOK BY ANY MECHANICAL, PHOTOGRAPHIC, OR ELECTRONIC PROCESS.

GLOSSARY & INDEX

NO PERMISSION HAS BEEN GRANTED BY N&N PUBLISHING COMPANY, INC TO REPRODUCE ANY PART OF THIS BOOK BY ANY MECHANICAL, PHOTOGRAPHIC, OR ELECTRONIC PROCESS.

NO PERMISSION HAS BEEN GRANTED BY N&N PUBLISHING COMPANY, INC TO REPRODUCE ANY PART OF THIS BOOK BY ANY MECHANICAL, PHOTOGRAPHIC, OR ELECTRONIC PROCESS.

NO PERMISSION HAS BEEN GRANTED BY N&N PUBLISHING COMPANY, INC TO REPRODUCE ANY PART OF THIS BOOK BY ANY MECHANICAL, PHOTOGRAPHIC, OR ELECTRONIC PROCESS.

NO PERMISSION HAS BEEN GRANTED BY N&N PUBLISHING COMPANY, INC TO REPRODUCE ANY PART OF THIS BOOK BY ANY MECHANICAL, PHOTOGRAPHIC, OR ELECTRONIC PROCESS.

NO PERMISSION HAS BEEN GRANTED BY N&N PUBLISHING COMPANY, INC TO REPRODUCE ANY PART OF THIS BOOK BY ANY MECHANICAL, PHOTOGRAPHIC, OR ELECTRONIC PROCESS.

NO PERMISSION HAS BEEN GRANTED BY N&N PUBLISHING COMPANY, INC TO REPRODUCE ANY PART OF THIS BOOK BY ANY MECHANICAL, PHOTOGRAPHIC, OR ELECTRONIC PROCESS.

NO PERMISSION HAS BEEN GRANTED BY N&N PUBLISHING COMPANY, INC TO REPRODUCE ANY PART OF THIS BOOK BY ANY MECHANICAL, PHOTOGRAPHIC, OR ELECTRONIC PROCESS.

Notes

NO PERMISSION HAS BEEN GRANTED BY N&N PUBLISHING COMPANY, INC TO REPRODUCE ANY PART OF THIS BOOK BY ANY MECHANICAL, PHOTOGRAPHIC, OR ELECTRONIC PROCESS.